Renewal of Marriage Vows

OPENING PRAYER

Priest. God our Father, guide of all people and ruler of creation, look upon these married couples who wish to confirm their offering of their marriage into your care.

As the years continue to pass by, help them to enter more deeply into their love for each other, and into the mystery of the Church.

We ask you this through Jesus Christ, Your Son, who lives and reigns with you and the Holy Spirit, one God, for ever and ever.

All: **Amen.**

FIRST READING
1 Corinthians 12:31 – 13:8a

A reading from the First Letter of St. Paul to the Corinthians.

Strive eagerly for the greatest spiritual gifts. But I shall show you a still more excellent way. If I speak in human and angelic tongues but do not have love, I am a resounding gong or a clashing cymbal. And if I have the gift of prophecy and comprehend all mysteries and all knowledge; if I have all faith so as to move mountains but do not have love, I am nothing. If I give away everything I own, and if I hand my body over so that I may boast but do not have love, I gain nothing.

Love is patient, love is kind. It is not jealous, love is not pompous, it is not inflated, it is not rude, it does not seek its own interests, it is not quick-tempered, it does not brood over injury, it does not rejoice over wrongdoing but rejoices with the truth. It bears all things, believes all things, hopes all things, endures all things. Love never fails.

Lector: The Word of the Lord!

All: **Thanks be to God!**

D0111734

Priest: The Lord be with you.

All: **And also with you.**

Priest: A reading from the holy gospel ✠ according to John.

All: **Glory to you, Lord!**

On the third day there was a wedding in Cana in Galilee, and the mother of Jesus was there. Jesus and his disciples were also invited to the wedding. When the wine ran short, the mother of Jesus said to him, "They have no wine." And Jesus said to her, "Woman, how does your concern affect me? My hour has not yet come." His mother said to the servers, "Do whatever he tells you."

Now there were six stone water jars there for Jewish ceremonial washings, each holding twenty to thirty gallons. Jesus told them, "Fill the jars with water." So they filled them to the brim. Then he told them, "Draw some out now and take it to the headwaiter." So they took it. And when the headwaiter tasted the water that had become wine, without knowing where it came from (although the servers who had drawn the water knew), the headwaiter called the bridegroom and said to him, "Everyone serves good wine first, and then when people have drunk freely, an inferior one; but you have kept the good wine until now."

Jesus did this as the beginning of his signs in Cana in Galilee and so revealed his glory, and his disciples began to believe in him.

Priest: The Gospel of the Lord!

All: **Praise to you, Lord Jesus Christ!**

INVITATION TO THE RENEWAL

Priest: Dear friends, on your wedding day you made a marriage covenant before God whereby you became husband and wife.

The future which lay before you, with its joys and sorrows, was hidden from your eyes. Yet you took each other for better or for worse, for richer or for poorer, in sickness and in health, till death should part you.

It is a beautiful tribute to your constant faith in each other that for all these years you have remained faithful to those pledges.

Today, with hearts full of gratitude, you have come here before this assembly to thank God for his great and merciful favors, and to renew the promises you made on your wedding day.

RENEWAL OF VOWS

Priest: Now, I ask each of you: Do you renew and confirm your taking of your spouse, here present, for your wedded mate?

All: **I do.**

Priest: Join your right hands and repeat your sacred pledge after me:

**I renew to you the promises I made to you
On our wedding day.**

**We have seen good times, and difficult times.
We have seen our love threatened,
and we have felt our love deepen.
I stand by you now,
and I will love you all the days of my life.**

BLESSING OF RINGS

Priest: Please hold up the hand on which you wear your wedding ring . . .

Lord, bless ✠ anew these rings and those who wear them.
Grant them unending faith in each other,
ever-deepening love through the years to come,
and peace in the fulfillment of your will.

We ask this through Christ our Lord.

All: **Amen.**

THE LORD'S PRAYER

Priest: Now, let us pray together, as Jesus taught us to pray . . .

Our Father . . .

BLESSING

Priest: May God the eternal Father keep you in love with each other, so that the peace of Christ may stay with you and be always in your home.

All: **Amen.**

Priest: May your children bless you, your friends console you, and all people live in peace with you.

All: **Amen.**

Priest: May you always bear witness to the love of God in this world so that the afflicted and the needy will find in you both generous friends, and welcome you in to the joys of heaven.

All: **Amen.**

Priest: And may almighty God bless you all, the Father ✠ and the Son, and the Holy Spirit.

All: **Amen.**

Renewal of Marriage Vows

OPENING PRAYER

Priest: God our Father, guide of all people and ruler of creation, look upon these married couples who wish to confirm their offering of their marriage into your care.

As the years continue to pass by, help them to enter more deeply into their love for each other, and into the mystery of the Church.

We ask you this through Jesus Christ, Your Son, who lives and reigns with you and the Holy Spirit, one God, for ever and ever.

All: **Amen.**

FIRST READING
1 Corinthians 12:31 – 13:8a

A reading from the First Letter of St. Paul to the Corinthians.

Strive eagerly for the greatest spiritual gifts. But I shall show you a still more excellent way. If I speak in human and angelic tongues but do not have love, I am a resounding gong or a clashing cymbal. And if I have the gift of prophecy and comprehend all mysteries and all knowledge; if I have all faith so as to move mountains but do not have love, I am nothing. If I give away everything I own, and if I hand my body over so that I may boast but do not have love, I gain nothing.

Love is patient, love is kind. It is not jealous, love is not pompous, it is not inflated, it is not rude, it does not seek its own interests, it is not quick-tempered, it does not brood over injury, it does not rejoice over wrongdoing but rejoices with the truth. It bears all things, believes all things, hopes all things, endures all things. Love never fails.

Lector: The Word of the Lord!

All: **Thanks be to God!**

GOSPEL

Priest: The Lord be with you.

All: **And also with you.**

Priest: A reading from the holy gospel ✠ according to John.

All: **Glory to you, Lord!**

On the third day there was a wedding in Cana in Galilee, and the mother of Jesus was there. Jesus and his disciples were also invited to the wedding. When the wine ran short, the mother of Jesus said to him, "They have no wine." And Jesus said to her, "Woman, how does your concern affect me? My hour has not yet come." His mother said to the servers, "Do whatever he tells you."

Now there were six stone water jars there for Jewish ceremonial washings, each holding twenty to thirty gallons. Jesus told them, "Fill the jars with water." So they filled them to the brim. Then he told them, "Draw some out now and take it to the headwaiter." So they took it. And when the headwaiter tasted the water that had become wine, without knowing where it came from (although the servers who had drawn the water knew), the headwaiter called the bridegroom and said to him, "Everyone serves good wine first, and then when people have drunk freely, an inferior one; but you have kept the good wine until now."

Jesus did this as the beginning of his signs in Cana in Galilee and so revealed his glory, and his disciples began to believe in him.

Priest: The Gospel of the Lord!

All: **Praise to you, Lord Jesus Christ!**

INVITATION TO THE RENEWAL

Priest: Dear friends, on your wedding day you made a marriage covenant before God whereby you became husband and wife.

The future which lay before you, with its joys and sorrows, was hidden from your eyes. Yet you took each other for better or for worse, for richer or for poorer, in sickness and in health, till death should part you.

It is a beautiful tribute to your constant faith in each other that for all these years you have remained faithful to those pledges.

Today, with hearts full of gratitude, you have come here before this assembly to thank God for his great and merciful favors, and to renew the promises you made on your wedding day.

RENEWAL OF VOWS

Priest: Now, I ask each of you: Do you renew and confirm your taking of your spouse, here present, for your wedded mate?

All: **I do.**

Priest: Join your right hands and repeat your sacred pledge after me:

**I renew to you the promises I made to you
On our wedding day.**

**We have seen good times, and difficult times.
We have seen our love threatened,
and we have felt our love deepen.
I stand by you now,
and I will love you all the days of my life.**

BLESSING OF RINGS

Priest: Please hold up the hand on which you wear your wedding ring . . .

Lord, bless ✠ anew these rings and those who wear them.
Grant them unending faith in each other,
ever-deepening love through the years to come,
and peace in the fulfillment of your will.

We ask this through Christ our Lord.

All: **Amen.**

THE LORD'S PRAYER

Priest: Now, let us pray together, as Jesus taught us to pray . . .

Our Father . . .

BLESSING

Priest: May God the eternal Father keep you in love with each other, so that the peace of Christ may stay with you and be always in your home.

All: **Amen.**

Priest: May your children bless you, your friends console you, and all people live in peace with you.

All: **Amen.**

Priest: May you always bear witness to the love of God in this world so that the afflicted and the needy will find in you both generous friends, and welcome you in to the joys of heaven.

All: **Amen.**

Priest: And may almighty God bless you all, the Father ✠ and the Son, and the Holy Spirit.

All: **Amen.**

11. *Visit to the Patriarchal Basilicas in Rome.*

A PLENARY INDULGENCE to those who devoutly visit one of the Patriarchal Basilicas in Rome and recite one Our Father and the Creed,

   1. On the titular feast of the Basilica;
   2. On any Holy Day of Obligation;
   3. Once a year on any other day of one's choice.

(Remember the three constants are also required to obtain ANY plenary indulgence.)

12. *PAPAL BLESSING.*

A PLENARY INDULGENCE is granted to those who "piously and devoutly" receive, even by radio, the Blessing of the Pope when imparted to Rome and the world (*Urbi et Orbi*). (3 constants.)

13. *Visit to a Cemetery.* Only applicable to the souls in Purgatory when one devoutly visits and prays for the departed. A PLENARY INDULGENCE is bestowed for this work each day between November 1 and November 8.

14. *Visit to a "Catacomb"* (early Christian cemetery.) Partial indulgence.

15. *Act of spiritual Communion* according to any pious formula – partial indulgence.

16. *Recitation of the Apostles Creed or the Nicene-Constantinopolian Creed* – partial indulgence.

17. *ADORATION OF THE CROSS.* A PLENARY INDULGENCE to those who in solemn liturgical action of Good Friday devoutly assist in at the adoration of the Cross and kiss it.

18. *Office of the dead.* A partial indulgence to those who devoutly recite Lauds or Vespers of the Office of the Dead.

19. *"Out of the Depths" (De profundis).* Psalm 129. Partial indulgence to those who recite.

20. *Christian Doctrine.* Partial indulgence to those who take part in teaching or learning Christian doctrine.

21. *"Lord God Almighty."* (Roman Breviary.) Partial indulgence.

22. *"Look down upon me, good and gentle Jesus."*
   "Look down upon me, good and gentle Jesus,
   while before your face I humbly kneel,
   and with burning soul pray and beseech you
   to fix deep in my heart lively sentiments of faith, hope and charity,
   true contrition for my sins,
   and a firm purpose of amendment,
   while I contemplate with great love and tender pity your five wounds,
   pondering over them within me,
   calling to mind the words which David, your prophet,

said of you, my good Jesus:
"They have pierced my hands and my feet;
they have numbered all my bones."
PLENARY INDULGENCE when recited on a Friday in Lent and Passiontide, when recited after Communion before an image of Christ crucified. On any other day the indulgence is partial.

23. *Eucharistic Congress.* PLENARY INDULGENCE to those who devoutly participate in the customary solemn eucharistic rite at the close of a Eucharistic Congress.

24. *"Hear Us"* (Roman Ritual) – partial indulgence.

25. *RETREAT. (Exercitia spiritualia).* PLENARY INDULGENCE to those who spend at least three (3) whole days in the spiritual exercises of a retreat.

26. *"Most sweet Jesus -- Act of Reparation"* PLENARY INDULGENCE when this prayer is publicly recited on the feast of the Most Sacred Heart of Jesus. Otherwise the indulgence is partial.

27. *"Most sweet Jesus, Redeemer – Act of Dedication of the Human Race to Jesus Christ King."* PLENARY INDULGENCE when this prayer is publicly recited on the feast of our Lord Jesus Christ King. Otherwise the indulgence is partial.

28. *The Moment of Death (In articulo mortis).* PLENARY INDULGENCE. EXCEPTION TO THE THREE CONSTANTS. (Verbatim recitation of the grant follows:)
"To the faithful in danger of death, who cannot be assisted by a priest to bring them the sacraments and impart the Apostolic Blessing with its plenary indulgence (see can. 468, Sec.2 of *Code of Canon Law*), Holy Mother Church nevertheless grants a plenary indulgence to be acquired at the point of death, provided they are properly disposed and have been in the habit of reciting some prayers during their lifetime. The use of a crucifix or a cross to gain this indulgence is praiseworthy.
"The condition: 'provided they have been in the habit of reciting some prayers during their lifetime' supplies in such cases for the three usual conditions required for the gaining of a plenary indulgence.
"The plenary indulgence at the point of death can be acquired by the faithful, even if they have already obtained another plenary indulgence on the same day."

29. *Litanies.* Partial indulgence to those who recite the following litanies: the litany of the Most Holy Name of Jesus; The litany of The Most Sacred Heart of Jesus; The litany of the Most Precious Blood of Our Lord Jesus Christ; The litany of the Blessed Virgin Mary; The litany of St. Joseph; and the litany of All Saints.

30. *"The Magnificat".* Partial indulgence.

31. *"Mary, Mother of Grace."* (Roman Ritual) Partial indulgence.

32. *"The Memorare."* (*Remember, O Most gracious Virgin Mary.*) Partial Indulgence.

33. *"The Miserere"* (*Have mercy on me.*) Psalm 50. Partial indulgence.

34. *Novena Devotions.* Partial indulgence to those who participate in a public novena before the feast of Christmas or Pentecost, or the Immaculate Conception.

35. *Use of Articles of Devotion.* (Verbatim follows:)
"The faithful, who devoutly use an article of devotion (crucifix or cross, rosary, scapular or medal) properly blessed by any priest, obtain a partial indulgence.
"But if the article of devotion has been blessed by the Sovereign Pontiff or by any Bishop, the faithful, using it, can also gain a PLENARY INDULGENCE on the feast of the Holy Apostles, Peter and Paul, provided they also make a profession of faith according to any legitimate formula."

36. *Little Offices.* The following Little Offices are each enriched with a partial indulgence: the Passion of our Lord Jesus Christ, the Most Sacred Heart of Jesus, the Immaculate Conception of the Blessed Virgin Mary, St. Joseph.

37. *Prayer for Sacerdotal or Religious Vocations.* Partial indulgence is granted to those who recite a prayer approved by ecclesiastical Authority for the above intention.

38. *Mental Prayer.* Partial indulgence to those who spend some time in pious mental prayer.

39. *"Let us pray for our Sovereign Pontiff"* (Roman Breviary) Partial Indulgence.

40. *"O Sacred Banquet"* (Roman Breviary) Partial indulgence.

41. *Assistance at Sacred Preaching.* PLENARY INDULGENCE is granted to those who attend a Mission, hear some of the sermons and are present for the solemn close of the Mission. A partial indulgence is granted to those who assist with devotion and attention at the sacred preaching of the Word of God.

42. *FIRST COMMUNION.* PLENARY INDULGENCE is granted to those who receive Communion for the first time or to those who ASSIST at the sacred ceremonies of a First Communion.

43. *First Mass of a Newly Ordained Priest.* PLENARY INDULGENCE granted to the priest and to the faithful who devoutly assist at the same Mass.

44. *"Prayer for Unity of the Church."* Partial indulgence.

45. *Monthly Recollection.* Partial indulgence to those who take part in a monthly retreat.

46. *"Eternal Rest."* A partial indulgence only to the souls in purgatory.
"Eternal rest grant to them, O Lord,
and let the perpetual light shine upon them.
May they rest in peace."

47. *"May it Please you, O Lord."* Partial indulgence.
"May it please you, O Lord,
to reward with eternal life
all those who do good to us for your Name's sake. Amen."

48. *RECITATION OF THE MARIAN ROSARY.* (The following is verbatim.)
"A PLENARY INDULGENCE is granted, if the Rosary is recited IN A CHURCH OR PUBLIC ORATORY OR IN A FAMILY GROUP, A RELIGIOUS COMMUNITY OR PIOUS ASSOCIATION; a partial indulgence is granted in other circumstances.

"Now the Rosary is a certain formula of prayer, which is made up of fifteen decades of 'Hail Marys' with an 'Our Father' before each decade, and in which the recitation of each decade is accompanied by pious meditation on a particular mystery of our Redemption.

"The name 'Rosary,' however, is commonly used in reference to only a third of the fifteen decades.

"The gaining of the plenary indulgence is regulated by the following norms:

"1) The recitation of a third part only of the Rosary suffices; but the five decades must be recited continuously.

"2) The vocal recitation MUST be accompanied by pious meditation on the mysteries.

"3) In public recitation the mysteries must be announced in the manner customary in the place; for private recitation, however, it suffices if the vocal recitation is accompanied by meditation on the mysteries.

"4) For those belonging to the Oriental rites, amongst whom this devotion is not practiced, the Patriarchs can determine some other prayers in honor of the Blessed Virgin Mary (for those of the Byzantine rite, for example, the Hymn *'Akathistos'* or the Office *'Paraclisis'*); to the prayers thus determined are accorded the same indulgences as for the Rosary."

49. *Jubilees of Sacerdotal Ordination.* A PLENARY INDULGENCE is granted to a priest on the 25th, 50th, and 60th anniversaries of his ordination when he renews before God his resolve to faithfully fulfill the duties of his vocation. If the priest celebrates a jubilee Mass, the faithful who assist at it can acquire a Plenary Indulgence.

50. *READING OF SACRED SCRIPTURE.*
While a partial indulgence is granted to those who read from Sacred Scripture with the veneration which the divine word is due, a PLENARY INDULGENCE is granted to those who read for at least one half an hour.

51. *"Hail Holy Queen."* (Roman Breviary.) Partial indulgence.

52. *"Holy Mary, help the helpless."* (Roman Breviary.) Partial indulgence.

53. *"Holy Apostles Peter and Paul."* (Roman Missal.) Partial indulgence.

54. *Veneration of the Saints.* Partial indulgence granted to those who on the feast of any Saint recite in his honor the oration of the Missal or any other approved by legitimate Authority.

55. *Sign of the Cross.* Partial indulgence.

56. *A Visit to the Stational Churches of Rome.*
A partial indulgence is granted to those who on the day indicated in the Roman Missal devoutly visit the stational church in Rome named for that day; but if they also assist at the sacred functions celebrated in the morning or evening, a PLENARY INDULGENCE is granted.

57. *"We fly to your Patronage."* Partial indulgence.

58. *Diocesan Synod.* PLENARY INDULGENCE is granted to those who during the time of a diocesan Synod, devoutly visit the church in which it is being held and there recite one Our Father and the Creed.

59. *"Down in Adoration Falling"* (*Tantum ergo*) (Roman Breviary) PLENARY INDULGENCE when recited on Holy Thursday and the feast of Corpus Christi. Otherwise a partial indulgence is granted for recitation.

60. *The Te Deum.* PLENARY INDULGENCE when recited publicly on the last day of the year. Otherwise a partial indulgence is granted to those who recite the *Te Deum* in thanksgiving.

61. *"Come, Holy Spirit, Creator Blest."* PLENARY INDULGENCE if recited on the first of January or on the feast of the Pentecost. Otherwise, a partial indulgence is granted to those who recite it.

62. *"Come, Holy Spirit"*
Come, Holy Spirit, fill the hearts of your faithful
and enkindle in them the fire of your love.
(Roman Missal) Partial indulgence.

63. *EXERCISE OF THE WAY OF THE CROSS.* PLENARY INDULGENCE. A Plenary indulgence is granted to those who piously make the Way of the Cross. The gaining of the indulgence is regulated by the following rules:
1. Must be done before stations of the cross legitimately erected.
2. 14 stations are required. Although it is customary for the icons to represent pictures or images, 14 simple crosses will suffice.
3. The common practice consists of fourteen pious readings to which some vocal prayers are added. However, nothing more is required than a pious meditation on the Passion and Death of the Lord, which need not be a particular consideration of the individual mysteries of the stations.
4. A movement from one station to the next is required. But if the stations are made publicly and it is not possible for everyone taking part to go from station to station, it suffices if at least the one conducting the exercise goes from station to station, the others remaining in their places.

Both indulgences can be acquired either on the day designated above or on some other day designated by the Ordinary (bishop) for the benefit of the faithful. The same indulgences apply to the Cathedral church and, where there is one, to a Co-Cathedral church, even if they are not parochial churches; they apply to quasi-parochial churches also.

66. *Visit to a Church or an Altar on the day of its consecration.* PLENARY INDULGENCE is granted to those who visit a church or an altar on the day itself of its consecration, and there recite on Our Father and the Creed.

67. *Visit to a Church or Oratory on All Souls Day.* PLENARY INDULGENCE. A plenary indulgence, applicable ONLY to the souls in purgatory, may be obtained by those who, on All Souls Day, piously visit a church, public oratory, or – for those entitled to use it – a semi-public oratory. It may be acquired either on the day designated as All Souls Day or, with the consent of the bishop, on the preceding or following Sunday or the feast of All Saints. On visiting the church or oratory it is required that one Our Father and the Creed be recited.

68. *Visit to a Church or Oratory of Religious on the Feast of the Holy Founder.* A PLENARY INDULGENCE is granted to those who piously visit a church or oratory of a religious order on the feastday of its canonized founder, and there recite one Our Father and the Creed.

69. *Pastoral Visitation.* Partial indulgence to those who visit a church during the time that a pastoral visitation is being held. But a PLENARY INDULGENCE, to be gained only once during the visitation, is granted if during the time of the visitation they assist at a sacred function at which the Visitator presides.

70. *Renewal of Baptismal Promises.* A partial indulgence is granted to those who renew their baptismal promises according to any formula in use; but a PLENARY INDULGENCE is granted if this is done in celebration of the Paschal Vigil or on the anniversary of one's baptism.

St. Agnes Cathedral

ROCKVILLE CENTRE, NEW YORK

Millennium Pilgrimage to the Holy Land

The Way of the Cross

Meditations of Pope John Paul II

Preparatory Prayer

Priest: My Lord, Jesus Christ . . .

All: . . . You have made this journey to die for me
with unspeakable love;
and I have so many times ungratefully abandoned You.
But now I love You with all my heart;
and, because I love You, I am sincerely sorry
for ever having offended You.
Pardon me, my God,
and permit me to accompany You on this journey.
You go to die for love of me;
I want, my beloved Redeemer, to die for love of You.
My Jesus, I will live and die always united to You.

THE CALM SOLEMNITY of the Passover meal had been disturbed by a
strong current of anxiety and apprehensiveness. The Master had in fact
said quite openly: "one of you is going to betray me." *Jn 13:21* And at
that moment Judas went out. *Jn 13:30* What is more, Jesus had said to
Peter: "You, this very night, before the cock crows twice, you will deny
me three times." *Mk 14:30-31* Yet Peter had declared himself willing to
die with him.

Gethsemane: a place of intense loneliness for Jesus, of almost total
withdrawal as he faced his Passion. It was a kind of bloodless foretaste
of the Passion. The inner reality of Jesus' agony in Gethsemane
remained hidden from his disciples, who, in any case, had fallen asleep
from emotional exhaustion. *Lk 22:45*

We must now move on from Jesus in his abandonment, his sweat
falling like drops of blood. But let us not forget that when he broke off
from prayer he said to Peter: "Watch and pray, so that you may not enter
into temptation...." *Mk 14:38*   Pope John Paul II.

At the cross her station keeping
Stood the mournful Mother weeping
Close to Jesus to the last.

The First Station
Pilate condemns Jesus to die

Priest: We adore You, O Christ, and we praise You.

All: **Because, by Your holy cross,
You have redeemed the world.**

Priest: Consider how Jesus Christ, after being scourged and crowned with thorns, was unjustly condemned by Pilate to die on the cross. *(Pause)*

PONTIUS PILATE'S VERDICT was pronounced under pressure from the priests and the crowd. "Crucify him! Crucify him!" *Jn 19:6* Pilate thought he could disassociate himself from the sentence by washing his hands, just as he had evaded what had been said by Christ – who identified his kingdom with the truth, with witness to the truth. *Jn 18:37* Pilate was trying to remain somehow "not involved." But the cross to which Jesus of Nazareth was condemned, like the truth he told about his kingdom, was to strike deep into Pilate's soul. One cannot remain uninvolved, on the side-lines.

When Jesus, the Son of God, was interrogated about his kingdom and, because of his kingdom was judged guilty by men and condemned to death, his final testimony began: he was about to demonstrate that "God loved the world so much...." *Jn 3:16*

We have this testimony before us, and we know that we are not allowed to wash our hands of it.   Pope John Paul II.

*Through her heart, His sorrow sharing
All His bitter anguish bearing
Now at length the sword has passed.*

The Second Station
Jesus accepts His cross

Priest: We adore You, O Christ, and we praise You.

All: **Because, by Your holy cross,
You have redeemed the world.**

Priest: Consider Jesus as He walked this road with the cross on His shoulders, thinking of us, and offering to His Father, in our behalf, the death He was about to suffer. *(Pause)*

THE EXECUTION, the implementation of the sentence, is beginning. Christ draws near to the cross, his body atrociously bruised and lacerated, blood trickling down his face from his head crowned with thorns. *Ecce homo!* In him there is all the truth foretold by the prophets about the Son of man, the truth predicted by Isaiah about the servant of Yahweh: "He was wounded for our iniquities ... in his wounds there is healing for us." *Is 53:5* And in him there is also an amazing sequel: here is what man had done to his God. Pilate says: *"Ecce homo!" Jn 19:5* – "Look what you have done to this man!" But there seems to be another voice speaking as well, a voice that seems to be saying: "Look what you have done, in this man, to your God!"

Pope John Paul II.

*O, how sad and sore distressed
Was that Mother highly blessed
Of the sole Begotten One.*

The Third Station
Jesus falls the first time

Priest: We adore You, O Christ, and we praise You.

All: **Because, by Your holy cross,**
You have redeemed the world.

Priest: Consider the first fall of Jesus. Loss of blood from the scourging and crowning with thorns had so weakened Him that He could hardly walk; and yet He had to carry that great load upon His shoulders. As the soldiers struck Him cruelly, He fell several times under the heavy cross. *(Pause)*

JESUS FALLS UNDER the weight of the cross. He falls to the ground. "Do you think that I cannot pray to my Father, who would at once send me more than twelve legions of angels?" *Mt 26:53* He does not ask for that. Having accepted the cup from his Father's hands *Mk 14:36* he is resolved to drink it to the end. He wills it no other way. "We had hoped," *Lk 24:21* the Emmaus disciples were to say a few days later. "If you are the Son of God...," *Mt 27:40* the members of the Sanhedrin were to fling at him. "He saved others but he cannot save himself," *Mt 27:42; Mk 15:31* the crowd was to yell.

And he accepts these provocations, which seem to undermine the whole meaning of his mission, his teaching, his miracles. He accepts them all, for he is determined not to combat them. He wills it all. To the end, down to the very last detail, he is true to his undertaking: "not my will but yours be done." *Mk 14:36*   Pope John Paul II.

Christ above in torment hangs
She beneath beholds the pangs
Of her dying, glorious Son.

The Fourth Station
Jesus meets His afflicted Mother

Priest: We adore You, O Christ, and we praise You.

All: **Because, by Your holy cross,
You have redeemed the world.**

Priest: Consider how the Son met His Mother on His way to Calvary. Jesus and Mary gazed at each other and their looks became as so many arrows to wound those hearts which loved each other so tenderly. *(Pause)*

THE MOTHER, MARY, meets her son along the way of the cross. His cross becomes her cross, his humiliation is her humiliation, the public scorn is on her shoulders. This is the way of the world. This is how it must seem to the people around, and this is how her heart reacts: "A sword will pierce your soul." *Lk 2:35* The words spoken when Jesus was forty days old are now coming true. They are reaching complete fulfillment.

Although the pain is proper to her, striking deep into her maternal heart, the full truth of this suffering can be expressed only in terms of shared suffering – *'com–passion.'* That word is part of the mystery; it expresses unity with the suffering of the Son.

Pope John Paul II.

*Is there one who would not weep,
'whelmed in miseries so deep
Christ's dear Mother to behold.*

The Fifth Station
Simon helps carry the cross

Priest: We adore You, O Christ, and we praise You.

**All: Because, by Your holy cross,
You have redeemed the world.**

Priest: Consider how weak and weary Jesus was. At each step He was at the point of expiring. Fearing that He would die on the way when they wished Him to die the infamous death of the cross, they forced Simon of Cyrene to help carry the cross after Our Lord. *(Pause)*

SIMON OF CYRENE, called upon to carry the cross, *Mk 15:21* doubtless had no wish to do so. When the condemned man's shoulders became too weak, he lent him his. *Lk 23:26* He moved along very close to Jesus, closer than Mary, closer than John who – though he too was a man – was not called upon to help. They called on him, Simon of Cyrene, father of Alexander and Rufus. They summoned him, they compelled him. *Mk 15:21*

How long did he go on resenting being forced into this?

We do not know. St. Mark simply records the names of the Cyrenian's sons, and tradition has it that they were members of the Christian community close to St. Peter. *Rom 16:13*   Pope John Paul II.

*Can the human heart refrain
From partaking in her pain
In that Mother's pain untold?*

The Sixth Station
Veronica offers her veil to Jesus

Priest: We adore You, O Christ, and we praise You.

All: **Because, by Your holy cross,**
You have redeemed the world.

Priest: Consider the compassion of the holy woman, Veronica. Seeing Jesus in such distress, His face bathed in sweat and blood, she presented Him with her veil. Jesus wiped His face, and left upon the cloth the image of His sacred countenance. *(Pause)*

TRADITION HAS BEQUEATHED us Veronica. Perhaps she is a counterpart to the story of the man from Cyrene. In obedience to the dictates of her heart, she wiped his face.

Tradition has it that an imprint of Christ's features remained on the handkerchief she used.

Yet, a different significance can be attributed to this detail if it is considered in the light of Christ's words about the final judgment. There will undoubtedly be many who will ask: "Lord, when did we ever do these things for you?" And Jesus will reply: "Whatever you did for the least of these brethren of mine, you did for me." *Mt 25:37-40* In fact, the Savior leaves his imprint on every single act of charity, as on Veronica's handkerchief.

Pope John Paul II.

Bruised, derided, cursed, defiled
She beheld her tender Child,
All with bloody scourges rent.

The Seventh Station
Jesus falls the second time

Priest: We adore You, O Christ, and we praise You.

All: **Because, by Your holy cross,
You have redeemed the world.**

Priest: Consider how the second fall of Jesus under His cross renews the pain in all the wounds of the head and members of our afflicted Lord. *(Pause)*

"I AM A WORM, not a man, scorned by all, the laughing-stock of the mob" *Ps 22:6* – the words of the Psalmist-prophet come wholly true in these steep, narrow little streets of Jerusalem in the last hours before the Passover. And we know that those hours before the feast are unnerving, with the streets teeming with people. This is the context in which the words of the Psalmist are coming true, even though nobody gives this a thought. Certainly it passes unnoticed by those who are displaying their scorn, people for whom this Jesus of Nazareth – who is now falling for the second time – has become a laughing-stock.

And he wills all this, he wills fulfillment of the prophecy. He falls the second time in accordance with his own will, so that "the scriptures may be fulfilled" *Mt 26:54* – "I am a worm, not a man."

Pope John Paul II.

*For the sins of His own nation
Saw Him hang in desolation
Till His spirit forth He sent.*

The Eighth Station
Jesus speaks to the women

Priest: We adore You, O Christ, and we praise You.

All: **Because, by Your holy cross,
You have redeemed the world.**

Priest: Consider how the women wept with compassion seeing Jesus so distressed and dripping with blood as he walked along. Jesus said to them, "Weep not so much for me, but rather for your children." *(Pause)*

HERE IS THE CALL to repentance, true repentance. Jesus says to the daughters of Jerusalem who are weeping at the sight of him: "Do not weep for me, but weep for yourselves and for your children." *Lk 23:28* One cannot merely scrape away at the surface of evil; one has to get down to its roots, its causes, the inner truth of the conscience.

This is the meaning of the Jesus who carries the cross. He must always be for us the nearest onlooker of all, the one who sees all our actions and is aware of all the verdicts passed on them by our consciences. He even makes us understand that these verdicts have to be carefully thought out, reasonable, objective (for he says "Do not weep"), but at the same time bound up with all that this truth contains; he warns us of this because he is the one who carries the cross.

Lord, let me know how to live and walk in the truth!

Pope John Paul II.

*O sweet Mother! Fount of Love,
Touch my spirit from above
Make my heart with yours accord.*

The Ninth Station
Jesus falls the third time

Priest: We adore You, O Christ, and we praise You.

All: **Because, by Your holy cross,
You have redeemed the world.**

Priest: Consider how Jesus Christ fell for the third time. He was extremely weak and the cruelty of His executioners was excessive; they tried to hasten His steps though He hardly had strength to move. *(Pause)*

EVERY STATION along this way is a milestone of obedience and self-deprivation.

We can appreciate the extent of that self-deprivation when we see Jesus falling for the third time under the cross. We can appreciate it when we think carefully who it is who is falling.

Who is it who has fallen? Who is Jesus Christ? "His nature was divine, yet he did not cling to his equality with God but preferred to deprive himself of it, taking the nature of a slave and becoming as men are; and after taking on human nature he became humbler still, making himself obedient even to death, death on a cross." *Phil 2:6-8*
Pope John Paul II.

*Make me feel as You have felt
Make my soul to glow and melt
With the love of Christ, my Lord.*

The Tenth Station
Jesus is stripped of His garments

Priest: We adore You, O Christ, and we praise You.

All: **Because, by Your holy cross, You have redeemed the world.**

Priest: Consider how Jesus was violently stripped of His clothes by His executioners. The inner garments adhered to His lacerated flesh and the soldiers tore them off so roughly that the skin came with them. *(Pause)*

WHEN JESUS is stripped of his clothes at Golgotha *Mk 15:24* our thoughts turn once again to his mother. They go back in time to the first days of this body which now, even before the crucifixion, is one mass of wounds. *Is 52:14* The mystery of the Incarnation: the Son of God derives his body from the Virgin's womb. *Mt 1:23; Lk 1:26-28* Christ's body expresses his love for the Father: "Then I said: See, I come . . . to do your will, O God." *Ps 40:7; Heb 10:7* "I always do what is pleasing to him." *Jn 8:29* With every wound, every spasm of pain, every wrenched muscle, every trickle of blood, with all the exhaustion in its arms, all the bruises and lacerations on its back and shoulders, this unclothed body is carrying out the will of both Father and Son.

At this station we must think of the Mother of Christ, because in her womb, before her eyes and at her hands the body of the Son of God was adored to the full.
Pope John Paul II.

Holy Mother, pierce me through
In my heart each wound renew
Of my Savior crucified.

The Eleventh Station
Jesus is nailed to the cross

Priest: We adore You, O Christ, and we praise You.

All: **Because, by Your holy cross,**
You have redeemed the world.

Priest: Consider Jesus, thrown down upon the cross, He stretched out His arms and offered to His eternal Father the sacrifice of His life for our salvation. They nailed His hands and feet, and then, raising the cross, left Him to die in anguish. *(Pause)*

"THEY HAVE PIERCED my hands and my feet, I can count all my bones." *Ps 22:16-17* The whole of this man is in a state of utmost tension: bones, muscles, nerves, every organ, every cell is stretched and strained to breaking-point. "I, when I am lifted up from the earth, will draw all men to myself." *Jn 12:32* Therein lies the full reality of the crucifixion. And part of this reality is the terrible tension driving its way into hands, feet, and every bone: driving its way into his entire body which, nailed like a mere thing to the beams of the cross, is about to be utterly 'voided' in the convulsive agony of death.

From the cross he says: "Father, forgive them, because they do not know what they are doing." *Lk 23:34*   Pope John Paul II.

Let me share with you His pain,
Who for all our sins was slain,
Who for me in torment died.

The Twelfth Station
Jesus dies upon the cross

Priest: We adore You, O Christ, and we praise You.

All: **Because, by Your holy cross, You have redeemed the world.**

Priest: Consider how your Jesus, after three hours of agony on the cross, is finally overwhelmed with suffering and, abandoning Himself to the weight of His body, bows His head and dies. *(Kneel)*

NAILED TO THE CROSS, pinned immobile in that terrible posture, Jesus invokes the Father. *Mk 15:34; Lk 23:46* All his invocations bear witness that he is one with the Father. "The Father and I are one." *Jn 10:30*

Here we have the finest, the most sublime work of the Son in union with the Father. Yes: in union, in the most perfect union possible, precisely at the moment when he cries: *"Eloi, Eloi, lama sabachthani"* – "My God, my God, why have you forsaken me?" *Mk 15:34* Those outstretched arms embrace all humanity and all the world.

Here is the man. Here is God himself. "In him we live and move and have our being." *Acts 17:28* In him: in those arms outstretched along the transverse beam of the cross. The mystery of redemption.

Pope John Paul II.

Let me mingle tears with thee
Mourning Him who mourned for me,
All the days that I may live.

The Thirteenth Station
Jesus is taken down from the cross

Priest: We adore You, O Christ, and we praise You.

All: **Because, by Your holy cross,
You have redeemed the world.**

Priest: Consider how, after Our Lord had died, He was taken down from the cross by two of His disciples, Joseph and Nicodemus, and placed in the arms of His afflicted Mother. She received Him with unutterable tenderness and pressed Him close to her bosom. *(Pause)*

WHEN THE BODY is taken down from the cross and laid in the Mother's arms, in our mind's eye we glimpse again the moment when Mary accepted the message brought by the Angel Gabriel: "You will conceive in your womb and give birth to a son whom you will call Jesus . . . the Lord God will give him the throne of David, his father . . . and his reign will never end." *Lk 1:31 33* All that Mary said was: "Let it all happen to me as you have said," *Lk 1:38* as though even then she had wanted to express what she is undergoing now.

Inseparable from this mystery is the extraordinary promise formulated by Simeon during the presentation of Jesus in the temple: "A sword will pierce your heart, so that the thoughts of many hearts may be laid bare." *Lk 2:35*

Once again Jesus is in her arms, as he was in the stable in Bethlehem. *Lk 2:16*   *Pope John Paul II.*

> *By the cross with you to stay*
> *There with you to weep and pray*
> *Is all I ask of you to give.*

The Fourteenth Station
Jesus is placed in the sepulcher

Priest: We adore You, O Christ, and we praise You.

All: **Because, by Your holy cross,**
You have redeemed the world.

Priest: Consider how the disciples carried the body of Jesus to its burial, while His holy Mother went with them and arranged it in the sepulcher with her own hands. They then closed the tomb and all departed. *(Pause)*

FROM THE MOMENT when man, because of sin, was banished from the tree of life, *Gn 3* the earth became a burial ground. For every human being there is a tomb. A vast planet of tombs.

Close to Calvary there was a tomb belonging to Joseph of Arimathea. In it, with Joseph's consent, the body of Jesus was placed after being taken down from the cross. *Mt 27:60; Mk 15:42-46* They laid it there in haste in order that the burial might be completed before the feast of Passover, which began at sunset. *Jn 19:31-42*

In one of the innumerable tombs scattered all over the continents of this planet of ours, the Son of God, the man Jesus Christ, conquered death with death.

All who look to the tomb of Jesus Christ live in Resurrection hope. *Pope John Paul II.*

Virgin of all virgins blest!
Listen to my fond request:
Let me share your grief divine.

On the Third Day . . .

THIS IS THE DAY the Lord has made. *Ps 118:24* God had already made this day his own in his wonderful work of creation. On that day God "rested," *Gn 2:2* and he commanded man to do likewise. *Gn 2:3; Ex 20:8-11* Then, once death had entered the world though man's disobedience, *Wis 2:24; Rom 5:12, 17, 19* God again made that day his own through his victory over death. *Is 25:8; 1 Cor 15:54-55; Rev 21:4* He is "not God of the dead but of the living." *Mt 22:32* So this is the day made by God, the Creator and the Lord of life.

"Look ... a spirit does not have flesh and bones as you see that I have," *Lk 24:39* he said to his disciples, astounded to see him enter that upper room. "Put your finger here and see my hands. Bring your hand closer and place it in my side," *Jn 20:27* Jesus said to Thomas who had said: "Unless I place my hand in his side I will not believe." *Jn 20:25-27* "Do not be skeptical, but believe!" said the risen Lord. And Thomas made his profession of faith, saying: "My Lord and my God." *Jn 20:28*

This is the day the Lord has made!   *Pope John Paul II.*

Prayer Before a Crucifix

Look down upon me,
good and gentle Jesus,
while before Your face I humbly kneel,
and with burning soul pray and beseech You
to fix deep in my heart
lively sentiments of faith, hope, and charity,
of true contrition for my sins,
and a firm purpose of amendment –
the while I contemplate
with great love and tender pity
Your five most precious wounds,
pondering over them within me,
and calling to mind the words
which David, Your prophet,
spoke of You, my Jesus:
*"They have pierced my hands and feet;
they have numbered all my bones."*

The faithful who, after receiving Communion, recite this prayer before a picture of Christ Crucified may gain a plenary indulgence on any Friday in Lent and a partial indulgence on other days on the year, with the addition of prayers for the Holy Father's intention.

Enchiridion Indulgentiarum – No. 22

The Stations of the Cross

URING THE TURKISH OCCUPATION of the Holy Land in the late Middle Ages, when pilgrims were prevented from visiting its sacred sites, the custom arose of making replicas of those holy places, where the faithful might come to pray. One of the most popular of these devotions was the "Stations of the Way of the Cross," which were imitations of the "stations," or stopping places of prayer on the Via Dolorosa in Jerusalem. By the late sixteenth century the fourteen stations, as we know them today, were erected in almost all Catholic churches.

Among the best known prayers for the Way of the Cross are those first published in Italian by St. Alphonsus Liguori in 1761, which are presented here in a new, revised translation. In his brief introduction to this devotion, St. Alphonsus wrote: "The pious exercise of the Way of the Cross represents the sorrowful journey that Jesus Christ made with the cross on His shoulders, to die on Calvary for the love of us. We should, therefore, practice this devotion with the greatest possible fervor, placing ourselves in spirit beside our Savior as He walked this sorrowful way, uniting our tears with His, and offering to Him both our compassion and out gratitude."

St. Agnes Cathedral

ROCKVILLE CENTRE, NEW YORK

INTRODUCTION TO INDULGENCES

You don't hear about indulgences anymore, at least not in Catholic circles. If it could be said that at one time they were over emphasized, it's surely true that today they're under-emphasized. Many Catholic simply don't know what indulgences are, and they're at a loss to explain the Church's position on indulgences when challenged by fundamentalists. And fundamentalists do bring up indulgences, perhaps because they know even less about them than the average, poorly-informed Catholic. There is surely no better place to turn than to the *Enchiridion of Indulgences*. *"Enchiridion"* means "handbook," and the *Enchiridion of Indulgences* is the Church's official handbook on what acts and prayers carry indulgences and what indulgences actually are. An indulgences is defined as "the remission before God of the temporal punishment due for sins already forgiven as far as their guilt is concerned." The first thing to note is that forgiveness of a sin is separate from punishment for the sin. Through sacramental confession we obtain forgiveness, but we aren't let off the hook as far as punishment goes.

Indulgences are two kinds: partial and plenary. A partial indulgences removes part of the temporal punishment due for sins. A plenary indulgence removes all of it. This punishment may come either in this life, in the form of various sufferings, or in the next life, in purgatory. What we don't get rid of here we suffer there.

TIME OFF FOR GOOD BEHAVIOR?

If you uncover a holy card or prayer book, you'll notice pious acts or recitation of prayers might carry an indication of time, such as "300 days" or "two years." Most fundamentalists, and even many Catholics, think such phrases refer to how much "time off for good behavior" you'd get in purgatory. If you perform a pious act labeled as "300 days' partial indulgence," then you'd spend 300 fewer days in purgatory. It's easy to see how misinformed Catholics might scurry around for years, toting up indulgences, keeping a little register in which they add up the days. "Let's see, last year's tally comes to one thousand three hundred twelve years, give or take a week or so, and my lifetime tally is now past the twenty thousand mark. I can cancel out a lot of sinning with this!" Or so some people might think. Well, there are no days or years in purgatory – or in heaven or hell, for that matter – and the indication of days or years attached to partial indulgences never meant you'd get that much time off in purgatory.

AS GOD SEES FIT

What it means was that you'd get a partial indulgence commensurate with what the early Christians got for doing penances for a certain length of time. But there has never been any way for us to measure how much "good time" that represents. All the Church could say, and all it ever did say, was that your temporal punishment would be reduced – as God saw fit. Since some Catholics were confused by the designation of days and years attached to partial indulgences, and since nearly all Protestants got a wrong idea of what those numbers meant, the rules for indulgences were modified in 1967, and now "the grant of a partial indulgence is designated only with the words "partial indulgence," without any determination of days or years," according to the *Enchiridion*.

To receive a partial indulgence, you have to recite the prayer or do the act of charity assigned. You have to be in the state of grace at least by the completion of the prescribed work. The rule says "at the completion" because often part of the prescribed work is going to confession, and you might not be in the state of grace before you do that. The other thing required is having a general intention to gain the indulgence. If you perform the required act but don't want to gain the indulgence, obviously you won't gain it.

The requirements for a plenary indulgence are tougher than for a partial. After all, a plenary indulgence remove all the temporal punishment due for the sins committed up to that time.

(If you sin later, of course, the temporal punishment connected with the new sins isn't covered by the earlier plenary indulgence, but, at least the punishment for the old sins isn't revived.)

"To acquire a plenary indulgence," says the *Enchiridion*, "it is necessary to perform the work to which the indulgence is attached and to fulfill the following three conditions: sacramental confession, Eucharistic Communion, and prayer for the intention of the Sovereign Pontiff. It is further required that all attachment to sin, even venial sin, be absent."

THE TOUGHEST REQUIREMENT

The greatest hurdle is the last. Making a good confession is not particularly difficult, and going to Communion and praying for the Pope's intentions are easier still. It's being free from all attachment to sin that's hard and it's quite possible that even evidently good people, who seek plenary indulgences regularly, never, in their whole lives, obtain one, because they are unwilling to relinquish their favorite little sins. There is an account of St. Philip Neri, who died in 1595, preaching a jubilee indulgence in a crowded church. A revelation was given to him that only two people in the church were actually getting it, an old char-woman and the saint himself. Not exactly encouraging, huh? But don't worry. If you aren't perfectly disposed and can't get the plenary indulgence. you'll at least come away with a partial.

It should be pointed out that the first three conditions may be fulfilled several days before or after doing the prescribed work, through receiving Communion and praying for the Pope are usually done the same day the work is performed.

By the way, the standard prayers for the Pope are one Our Father and one Creed, though you're at liberty to substitute other prayers.

VARIOUS GRANTS

The bulk of the *Enchiridion* is a listing of indulgenced prayers and acts. First come three "general grants."

The first says "a partial indulgence is granted to the faithful who, in the performance of their duties and in bearing the trials of life, raise their mind with humble confidence to God, adding – even if only mentally – some pious invocation." It is noted that this grant "is intended to serve as an incentive to the faithful to practice the commandment of Christ that `they must always pray and not lose heart'" [Luke 18:1]

The second general grant is this: "A partial indulgence is granted to the faithful who, in a spirit of faith and mercy, give of themselves or of their goods to serve their brothers in need." This grant "is intended to serve as an incentive to the faithful to perform more frequent acts of charity and mercy," as Christ commanded [John 13:15, Acts 10:38]. The third general grant provides that "a partial indulgence is granted to the faithful who, in a spirit of penance, voluntarily deprive themselves of what is licit and pleasing to them." This provision is meant "to move the faithful to bridle their passions and thus to bring to their bodies into subjection and to conform themselves to Christ in his poverty and suffering" [Matt 8:20, Matt 16:24].

PROVISIONS

After the discussion of the general grants comes a listing of miscellaneous prayers and acts to which indulgences are attached. This list is much shorter than in former years, the Church having decided to limit indulgences to the most important works.

There is no room or need to mention all the pious acts which are indulgenced, but it's worth noting that a plenary indulgence is given for the recitation of the rosary in a church or family group (and not just the recitation, of course, but the fulfilling of the usual conditions for a plenary indulgence).

Likewise, first communicants and those who "assist at the sacred ceremonies of a First Communion – for example, the parents – can receive a plenary indulgence. And the same reward is given to those who, "with the veneration due the divine word, make a spiritual reading from Sacred Scripture" for at least half an hour. Even making the Sign of the Cross has a partial indulgence attached to it.

NORMS

Norm 1. An indulgence is the remission before God of the temporal punishment due sins already forgiven as far as their guilt is concerned, which the follower of Christ with the proper dispositions and under certain determined conditions acquires through the intervention of the Church which, as minister of the Redemption, authoritatively dispenses and applies the treasury of the satisfaction won by Christ and the saints.

Norm 2. And indulgence is partial or plenary according as it removes either part or all of the temporal punishment due sin.

Norm 3. Partial as well as plenary indulgences can always be applied to the dead by way of suffrage.

Norm 4. A partial indulgence will henceforth be designated only with the words "partial indulgence" without any determination of days or years.

Norm 5. The faithful who at least with a contrite heart perform an action to which a partial indulgence is attached obtain, in addition to the remission of temporal punishment acquired by the action itself, an equal remission of punishment through the intervention of the Church.

Norm 6. A plenary indulgence can be acquired only once a day, except for the provisions contained in No. 18 for those who are on the point of death. A partial indulgence can be acquired more than once a day, unless there is an explicit indication to the contrary.

Norm 7. To acquire a plenary indulgence it is necessary to perform the work to which the indulgence is attached and to fulfill three conditions: sacramental confession, Eucharistic Communion and prayer for the intentions of the Supreme Pontiff. It is further required that all attachment to sin, even to venial sin, be absent. If this disposition is in any way less than complete, or if the prescribed three conditions are not fulfilled, the indulgence will be only partial, except for the provisions contained in No. 11 for those who are "impeded."

Norm 8. The three conditions may be fulfilled several days before or after the performance of the prescribed work; nevertheless it is fitting that Communion be received and the prayers for the intentions of the Supreme Pontiff be said the same day the work is performed.

Norm 9. A single sacramental confession suffices for gaining several plenary indulgences, but Communion must be received and prayers for the Supreme Pontiff's intentions recited for the gaining of each plenary indulgence.

Norm 10. The condition of praying for the Supreme Pontiff's intentions is fully satisfied by reciting one Our Father and one Hail Mary; nevertheless the individual faithful are free to recite any other prayer according to their own piety and devotion toward the Supreme Pontiff.

Norm 11. While there is no change in the faculty granted by canon 935 of the Code of Canon Law to confessors to commute for those who are "impeded" either the prescribed work itself or the required conditions [for the acquisition of indulgences], local Ordinaries can grant to the faithful over whom they exercise authority in accordance with the law, and who live in places where it is impossible or at least very difficult for them to receive the sacraments of confession and Communion, permission to acquire a plenary indulgence without confession and Communion provided they are sorry for their sins and have the intention of receiving these sacraments as soon as possible.

Norm 12. The division of indulgences into "personal," "real' and "local" is abolished so as to make it clearer that indulgences are attached to the actions of the faithful even though at times they may be linked with some object or place.

Norm 13. The *"Enchridion of Indulgences"* is to be revised with a view to attaching indulgences only to the most important prayers and works of piety, charity and penance.

Norm 14. The list and summaries of indulgences special to religious orders, congregations, societies of those living in community without vows, secular institutes and the pious associations of faithful are to be revised as soon as possible in such a way that plenary indulgences may be acquired only on particular days established by the Holy See acting on the recommendation of the Superior General, or in the case of pious associations, of the local Ordinary.

Norm 15. A plenary indulgence applicable only to the dead can be acquired in all churches and public oratories – and in semipublic oratories by those who have the right to use them – on November 2. In addition, a plenary indulgence can be acquired twice a year in parish churches; on the feast of the church's titular saint and on August 2, when the *"Portiuncula"* occurs, or on some other more opportune day determined by the Ordinary.

All the indulgences mentioned above can be acquired either on the days established or – with the consent of the Ordinary – on the preceding or the following Sunday. Other indulgences attached to churches and oratories are to be revised as soon as possible.

Norm 16. The work prescribed for acquiring a plenary indulgence connected with a church or oratory consists in a devout visit and the recitation of one Our Father and the Creed.

Norm 17. The faithful who use with devotion an "object of piety" (crucifix, cross, rosary, scapular or medal) properly blessed by any priest, can acquire a partial indulgence. But if this "object of piety" is blessed by the Supreme Pontiff or any bishop, the faithful who use it devoutly can also acquire a plenary indulgence on the feast of the holy Apostles Peter and Paul, provided they also make a profession of faith using any legitimate formula.

Norm 18. To the faithful in danger of death who cannot be assisted by a priest to bring them the sacraments and impart the apostolic blessing with its attendant plenary indulgence (according to canon 468, sec.2 of the *Code of Canon Law*) Holy Mother Church nevertheless grants a plenary indulgence to be acquired at the point of death (*in articulo mortis*), provided they are properly disposed and have been in the habit of reciting some prayers during their lifetime. To use a crucifix or cross in connection with the acquisition of this plenary indulgence is a laudable practice. This plenary indulgence at the point of death can be acquired by the faithful even if they have already obtained another plenary indulgence on the same day.

Norm 19. The norms established regarding plenary indulgences, particularly those referred to in N.6, apply also to what up to now have been known as the "*toties quoties*" ["as often as"] plenary indulgences.

Norm 20. Holy Mother Church, extremely solicitous for the faithful departed, has decided that suffrages be applied to them to the widest possible extent at any Sacrifice of the Mass whatsoever, abolishing all special privileges in this regard.

INDULGENCED WORKS

THE ENCHIRIDION OF INDULGENCES
Issued by the Sacred Apostolic Penitentiary, 1968

✠ JOSEPH CARDINAL FERRETTO,
Titular Bishop of the Suburban Church of Sabina and Poggio Mirteto

Originally published by *Liberia Editrice Vaticana*, Vatican City, 1968

This is a digest of the works and prayers listed in the Enchiridion of Indulgences. The Enchiridion recites each indulgenced prayer in full. Because most are recognizable they will only be listed by name. The un-translated Enchiridion lists each work and prayer in alphabetical order by their Latin names. The order shall remain the same in this listing. The descriptions of the works and details regarding obtaining the indulgence will be edited and abbreviated in this listing. The following is not represented to be an exact reprint of the Enchiridion but and accurate digest of what constitutes an approved indulgenced work by the Sacred Apostolic Penitentiary.

In all but the plenary indulgence of *In Articulo Mortis*, at the moment of death, a plenary indulgence mentioned below MUST be accompanied by the three prerequisites of a plenary indulgence.
- Sacramental Confession,
- Communion, and
- Prayer for the intention of the Holy Father, all to be performed within days of each other if not at the same time.

Thus the formula for obtaining a plenary indulgence are the three constants mentioned above plus any one of the variable works mentioned below as being worthy of a plenary indulgence.

1. *Direct, we beg you, O Lord.* (Prayer from Roman Ritual) Partial indulgence.

2. *Acts of the Theological Virtues and of Contrition.* A partial indulgence is granted to those who devoutly recite, according to any legitimate formula, the acts of faith, hope, charity, and contrition.

3. *ADORATION OF THE MOST BLESSED SACRAMENT.*
A PLENARY INDULGENCE is granted to those who visit the Most Blessed Sacrament for at least one half hour (together with the three prerequisites (constants) of a plenary indulgence. A partial indulgence is granted to those who visit and adore the Most Blessed Sacrament without the three constants or for any period less than one half hour.

4. *Hidden God (Adoro te devote)* – hymn, partial indulgence.

5. *We have come (Adsumus)* – prayer, partial indulgence.

6. *To you, O blessed Joseph (Ad te, beate Ioseph)* – prayer, partial indulgence.

7. *We Give You Thanks* – prayer from Roman Breviary, partial indulgence.

8. *Angel Of God* – prayer, partial indulgence.

9. *The Angel Of The Lord* – prayer, partial indulgence.

10. *Soul of Christ (Anima Christi)* – prayer, partial indulgence.

THE PILGRIM'S NEW GUIDE
TO THE HOLY LAND

The Pilgrim's New Guide to the Holy Land

SECOND EDITION

Stephen C. Doyle, O.F.M.

A Michael Glazier Book
THE LITURGICAL PRESS
Collegeville, Minnesota

A Michael Glazier Book published by The Liturgical Press

Cover design by David Manahan, O.S.B. Cover photos courtesy of COREL Photos.

Photo on page 86 by Hugh Witzmann, O.S.B.
Other photos from COREL Photos. Reprinted with permission.

The English translation of the General Intercession VI for Good Friday from *The Sacramentary* © 1974, 1985, International Committee on English in the Liturgy, Inc. All rights reserved.

2	3	4	5	6	7	8

ISBN 0-8146-5955-1

Contents

PART II

Holy Places East of Jerusalem

PART III

Holy Places West of Jerusalem

Appendices and Index

Acknowledgments

The author wishes to acknowledge and thank the following: Fr. Walter Abbott, S.J., for quotes from the Documents of Vatican II; the Daughters of St. Paul for quotes from Paul VI's "On Evangelization"; Most Rev. J. Terry Steib, S.V.D., for his meditation on the church; Bruce Barton for "There Are Two Seas"; and the Poor Clares of Nazareth for the "Prayer of Abandonment" of Charles de Foucald. The hymns are reprinted with the permission of the copyright holders or their representatives.

Preface
to the Second Edition

It has been very gratifying to learn how many pilgrims have been able to change a tourist trip into a pilgrimage because of this book. I first wrote it precisely because of the tales of disappointment I heard from those who went to the Holy Land seeking a spiritual experience, only to have been sidetracked into shopping sprees, nationalistic forays, or a blitzkrieg of facts about Herodian walls, Bronze Age cisterns, Philistine pottery and Hasmonean reconstruction. Shopping, national pride, and archaeology will have a valid place in every pilgrimage.

However, there are major differences between going to the Holy Land as a pilgrim, and going there as a tourist, or even as a student of history or archaeology. One joins a pilgrimage from faith and for faith. This is not the same as a deepening of theological insight, or becoming more knowledgeable about the facts and beliefs of Christianity. The first Eucharistic Prayer speaks of "Abraham, Our Father in faith." He is the ancestor of Jew, Moslem, and Christian; indeed, of all who call that land "HOLY." Impelled by faith and "seeking the face of God," he heard the voice of God. (In Hebrew to hear is the same word as to obey: "shamah"). "Go forth from the land of your kinsfolk and from your father's house to a land that I will show you" (Gen 12:1).

As a pilgrim in the Holy Land, you join Abraham, Mary, the Mother of Jesus, Paul, Francis of Assisi, Ignatius of Loyola, and Paul VI. They have made the yearning of Paul their own pilgrim's prayer. *"Father, I consider everything as a loss because of the supreme good of knowing Christ Jesus my Lord. For his sake I have let go of all things and I consider them so much rubbish, that I may gain Christ . . . I continue my journey in hope*

*that I may possess (him) since I have been taken hold of by (him) . . . for-
getting what lies behind but straining to what lies ahead, I continue my
pursuit toward the goal, the heavenly prize which beckons, God's call in
Christ Jesus"* (Phil 3:8-14 passim). Therein lies the major difference between a tour and a pilgrimage.

For Christian pilgrims, Jesus is their companion to the places made
holy by his life, and he is also the goal of the pilgrimage. Luke's Gospel
depicts the Lord's whole life as a journey to Jerusalem. The Letter to the
Hebrews describes how, having completed his own earthly pilgrimage, he
beckons those who are still on theirs: *". . . let us rid ourselves of every
burden and sin that clings to us and persevere in running the race (read
pilgrimage) that lies before us while keeping our eyes fixed on Jesus, the
leader and perfecter of faith. For the sake of the joy that lay before him he
endured the cross, despising its shame, and has taken his seat at the right
of the throne of God"* (Heb 12:1-3).

This basic vision that distinguishes a pilgrim from a tourist is summed
up in another passage by Paul: *"Since you have accepted Christ Jesus as
Lord, sink your roots deep in him, build your faith upon him, and overflow
with thanksgiving"* (Col 2:6).

This book tries to bring together those things that will facilitate that
vision.

1. A brief introduction to each Holy Place is given. Detailed descriptions, facts, and details can be found in other guide books.

2. The Scripture passages appropriate to the location are provided. On
the lecture circuit one of the most frequently asked questions is "Which is
the best translation of the Bible?" I usually reply: The Revised New American Bible, The New Revised Standard Version, The New Jerusalem Bible,
The Revised International Version, etc., etc. They are all good but none of
them conveys completely and perfectly the meaning and nuance of the
original Hebrew, Aramaic, or Greek. That is impossible, but the attempt
must always be made anew. Notice that each of the versions made in the
last half century is either new or revised in the last decade or so.

Rev. Kenneth Bailey, a great Christian and biblical scholar, and my
neighbor at the Tantur Ecumenical Institute near Bethlehem, constantly re-
minds his audiences that the word of the Bible was made flesh in the East.
To read it only from a Western perspective may well miss what God is saying to us through the human word. He further emphasizes that Jesus was a
practitioner of the "new theology." That presumes a knowledge of the "old
theology" that Jesus tried and found wanting, and an openness to what
may be his surprising and even shocking insights. Another of his counsels

is that we should presume that many of the biblical texts have become too familiar to us so that we have lost their full impact and deepest meaning. Solution: step back and try to hear them from a new point of view.

In a similar vein, Pius XII in 1943 told us that to ascertain the meaning of God's word, we must go back to the original languages, ascertain the intention of the author, and take into account the literary form. Following these suggestions, *the biblical passages in this guide are my own translation*. Fools walk in where angels fear to tread, and I am no angel. Yet, I dare to hope and pray that these translations (sometimes paraphrases) done for a new experience, in a new context, in a new culture may provide new insights that we will carry back to the familiarity of our own churches and translations of the word.

3. New to this edition are the insights gleaned from Documents of Vatican II, Paul VI's Decree on Evangelization, and prose and poetry that offer insights and foster the spirit of prayer.

4. Hymns. Only the words of hymns are provided, with the understanding that it is a rare group that will have a director of music, able to teach the ones that are not known. Hopefully most of the hymns chosen will be familiar. They are found in the special music section with an important exception. At the stations on the Via Dolorosa where juggling pages would be inconvenient, the words are included in the body of the text.

5. The number of times I have been a pilgrim with groups in the Holy Land surpassed one hundred some time ago. This book is heavily dependent upon their faith, experience, and insights. I do not share the sentiments of the author of the book of Revelation: "If anyone adds to the prophetic word of this book, God will get them. If anyone deletes any of the prophetic words of this book, the Almighty will delete them from the tree of life and the Holy City." I would be happy to hear of any additions or deletions that you believe might be an improvement to this guide. I do, however, concur with the author's final sentiments: "The One who is witness of all of these things says: I am coming soon. Amen: come Lord Jesus! May the grace of Our Lord Jesus Christ abide with you."

Stephen Clare Doyle, O.F.M.
Franciscan Pilgrimages
St. Anthony Shrine
100 Arch Street
Boston, MA 02110
Fax 617-542-4225

A Pilgrim's Prayer

Lord Jesus, your feet made this land holy.
You came as a pilgrim to this City of Peace.
As we follow your steps
Open our eyes that we may see.
May we see you not only in the stones,
but in your people and each other.
Write your Gospel in our hearts.
Help us to proclaim it with our lives.
Lord, each day as we follow you to the heavenly Jerusalem,
teach us to pray as you taught those who first followed you.

Our Father, who art in heaven, hallowed be thy name. Thy Kingdom come, thy will be done on earth as it is in heaven. Give us this day our daily bread, and forgive us our trespasses as we forgive those who trespass against us. And lead us not into temptation but deliver us from evil. For thine is the kingdom, the power and the glory forever and ever. Amen.

Part I

Jerusalem, Jerusalem

Jerusalem, Jerusalem

CHRONOLOGY

Key Dates in the History of the Holy Land

Prehistoric Times: Our ancestors known as "Mount Carmel Men" inhabited caves at the foot of Mount Carmel. (One of the skeletons was found with an arrow head imbedded in it!) The Jordan Rift Valley continues into Africa where it becomes the Ulduvai Gorge, the scene of dramatic finds from pre-history, by the Leakey family.

Circa 1750 B.C.: Abraham, our father in faith, becomes the first pilgrim in the land of Canaan and makes a mutual protection treaty with Melchizedek, king and priest of Jerusalem (Gen 14:18-20; cf. Hebrews 7).

Circa 1250 B.C.: Moses is chosen by Yahweh (the divine name revealed in the burning bush) to lead the children of Israel from the slavery of Egypt to the covenant of being God's chosen people at Sinai (Exodus 19 and 1 Peter 2).

Circa 1200 B.C.: After the death of Moses on Mount Nebo on the other side of the Jordan from Jericho, Joshua leads the people into the "Promised Land" and renews the covenant (Joshua 24). For about one hundred and fifty years the twelve tribes are united in a loose confederation under the sporadic leadership of the "Judges."

Circa 1050 B.C.:   The repetition of the refrain "At that time there was no king in Israel and every one did what they thought best" (Judg 7:6; 18:1; 19:1; 21:25) signals the need for a new form of government. With ill-concealed reluctance Samuel, the last of the Judges, anoints (Heb: mashah) the first "messiah," Saul.

Circa 1000 B.C.:   David becomes the ideal messiah (1 Samuel 16), takes the Canaanite city of Jerusalem as his capital, its priest Zadok as his chaplain, and makes it the focal point of worship by installing the Ark of the Covenant there. The task of building a "house" for Yahweh there is left for his son, Solomon. Instead, Yahweh promises to build the "house of David" (2 Samuel 5–7).

Circa 950 B.C.:   Solomon builds a retaining wall around Mount Moriah, just to the north of the city of David (also called Jerusalem or Zion), fills it in to form a plateau upon which he builds the House of Yahweh. In front of it, the stone peak of Mount Moriah (now inside the Dome of the Rock) becomes the foundation of the altar of holocausts. Upon the death of Solomon his son Rehoboam is left as the ruler of the two southern tribes of Judah and Benjamin. Under Jeroboam, the ten tribes of the north separate and form the nation of Israel with their capital in Samaria (1 Kings 12).

722–721 B.C.:   The prediction of Isa 7:14 (the Emmanuel oracle) is fulfilled when Israel is conquered by Assyria which deports the ten tribes, giving rise to the legends of the "Lost ten tribes of Israel."

701 B.C.:   The same fate is avoided by the Kingdom of Judah under the messiah, Hezekiah, who defends Jerusalem against the Assyrians with his famous tunnel and wall, averting the "destruction of Sennacharib."

587 B.C.:   The Babylonian exile follows the destruction of the Temple and the Holy City after the warnings of Jeremiah are ignored. In the exile Yahweh reveals his will (original meaning of Torah) in the preaching of Ezekiel and the message of the anonymous prophet known as Deutero-Isaiah (Isaiah 40–55). The Bible is

born through the literary activity of the priests who, deprived of their liturgical function without a temple, revert to their original vocation: "the Levites keep your words, and your covenant they up-hold" (Deut 33:9).

537 B.C.: After defeating the Babylonians, Cyrus the Persian permits the Jews to return from exile and rebuild the Holy City and the Temple (Isaiah 45). A sizable number does not return, believing that being a member of God's chosen people, a Jew, involves hearing the word, not the place where it is done. Their fidelity and prayer eventually produce the "Babylonian Talmud," still a beacon in the spiritual life of the observant Jew. The returning exiles produced a companion commentary on the word, called the "Jerusalem Talmud."

330 B.C.: Alexander the Great replaces the Persian rule in the Holy Land with his Greek empire. Upon his death his empire is divided among his generals. Ptolemy in Egypt also rules the Holy Land until around the year 200 when he loses it to the descendants of Alexander's General Antiochus in Syria.

167–164 B.C.: The Syrian, Antiochus IV, styles himself "Epiphanes" (the manifestation of God), imposes his program of Hellenization, puts up a statue of himself (the "Abomination of the Desolation") in the Temple's Holy of Holies, and demands sacrifice to it under pain of death. A priestly family, the Maccabees (later called the Hasmoneans), leads a successful three-and-a-half year revolt. Their success is crowned with the rededication of the temple and the relighting of the lights on the Menorah, giving rise to the feast of Hanukkah (cf. 1 and 2 Maccabees).

68 B.C.: Hasmonean Civil War provides the opportunity for Roman intervention under Pompey. The autonomous Jewish state, lasting less than one hundred years, does not rise again until 1948 (except for the aborted revolt of Simon bar Cochba. [A.D. 132–135]).

39 B.C.: Herod the Great, of mixed Jewish and Idumean parentage, is appointed king by the Roman senate. His cruelty

was unbounded. To legitimize his position, he marries Mariamne, the last of the direct line of the Hasmoneans. Then, to prevent his descendants from being considered Hasmonean, he murders her and the sons she bore him. His incredibly ambitious building projects include a memorial tower to her in Jerusalem.

5–4 B.C.:

Toward the end of Herod's cruel reign, Jesus Christ, the Son of God was born of the virgin Mary in Bethlehem. (Christian calculation of the years back to the birth of Jesus was in error.)

A.D. 29:

Jesus, the Messiah offers himself as a sacrifice of love (John 10:11-18) on a skull-shaped hill in a quarry outside the walls of the Holy City. He rose and ascended to his Father where he "is still our High priest, our advocate who always pleads our cause" (Preface III of Easter). The Church is born with the sending of the Holy Spirit to continue the work of its Lord (John 20:21-2).

A.D. 40–44:

Herod Agrippa, grandson of Herod the Great, sensing that the Romans may attack to smother the brush fires of the Zealots' revolt, builds the Third Wall, thus enclosing Calvary within the city.

A.D. 66–70:

The first Jewish revolt ends with the destruction of the city and the temple on the same day as the Temple of Solomon was destroyed in 587 B.C. (The commemoration in late summer takes its name from the date of the dual destruction in the Lunar calendar: Tisha b' Av, Ninth of Av.) An early tradition has it that the Jerusalem Christian community survived by fleeing to Pella in Trans-Jordan, southeast of the Sea of Galilee.

A.D. 132–135:

The second Jewish revolt was occasioned by Emperor Hadrian's decision to build a pagan city, Aelia Capitolina, on the ruins of the Holy City. His plan was eventually achieved, but not before Shimeon bar Cochba and his Jewish army kept the power of Rome at bay for three years. The Roman Province was officially named Syria Palestina or Palestine after the Philistines, or the peoples of the Sea who settled along the coastal plain around the same time the Israelites were entering into the land after the Exodus.

A.D. 325:   Constantine establishes a second capital for the empire at Byzantium (the origin of the symbol of the two-headed imperial eagle), and calls it Constantinople. He establishes Christianity as the religion of the empire, and the east becomes politically subject to the emperor, and ecclesiastically subject to the patriarch, both with headquarters at Byzantium, hence, the Byzantine Empire and Church. St. Helena, the emperor's mother, ascertains from the local community the sacred places of Bethlehem and Jerusalem, and marks the birth and resurrection of the Lord with magnificent churches.

A.D. 614:   The Persians invade and leave all the churches in shambles with the exception of Bethlehem which they spare when they see the mosaics of the Magi in Persian dress on the facade.

A.D. 638:   Six years after the death of the prophet Mohammed, his successor, the Caliph Omar enters Jerusalem, ending Byzantine rule over the Holy Land. For the next thirteen hundred years, interrupted by less than a century of the crusader kingdom, the city is in the hands of the Moslems who call it El Quds, "The Holy." It ranks after Mecca and Medina among the Holy Places of Islam.

A.D. 1009:   The mad caliph Hakim profanes the Holy Places and destroys the churches. Sixty years later the Seljuk Turks cut off access to the Holy Places, precipitating Pope Urban II's call for a crusade in 1095.

A.D. 1099:   Jerusalem falls to the "Franks," as the Crusaders are called, and the Latin Kingdom of Jerusalem is established. The Patriarch of Jerusalem is no longer an eastern bishop from Constantinople, but a Latin bishop from Rome.

A.D. 1187:   At the battle of the Horns of Hattin on July 4, Saladin soundly defeats the Crusaders and then routs them at

Nazareth, Tabor, and Jerusalem. For another century they retain a foothold at Acco (St. Jean d'Acre).

A.D. 1219:   Francis of Assisi arrives for a pilgrimage, and leaves some of his little brothers (Friars Minor) to bear witness to the gospel and assist pilgrims. The Franciscan Custody of the Holy Land is born.

A.D. 1517:   Under Suleiman the Magnificent, the Turks (the Ottoman Empire) rule until 1918. He lavishly adorned the Holy City, encircling it with the walls that enclose it today.

A.D. 1895:   Theodore Herzl, a Viennese journalist covering the Dreyfus trial in France with its virulent anti-Semitism and contemporaneous pogroms in Russia, concludes that without their own country, Jews are not safe. He is the father of political Zionism, the movement for a homeland for the Jewish people. Waves of Jewish immigration (Aliya) begin.

A.D. 1919:   Turkey allied with the losing side in the First World War. At its conclusion, the victors dismembered the Ottoman Empire, and the League of Nations gave Great Britain a mandate over Palestine. The Balfour declaration of the British Foreign Office declared "His Majesty's Government is not opposed to the establishment of a homeland for the Jewish people in Palestine."

A.D. 1948:   After a favorable vote in the United Nations, the state of Israel is established. Every neighboring Arab nation declares war on the Jewish state and the Palestinian refugee problem begins.

A.D. 1967:   Israel wins the Six-Day War and occupies the Old City of Jerusalem, the West Bank (the area occupied by Jordan in 1948), the Golan Heights (Syria), and the Sinai (Egypt). The search for justice and peace for all continues.

Pray for the peace of Jerusalem.

Map of Israel, The Occupied Territories

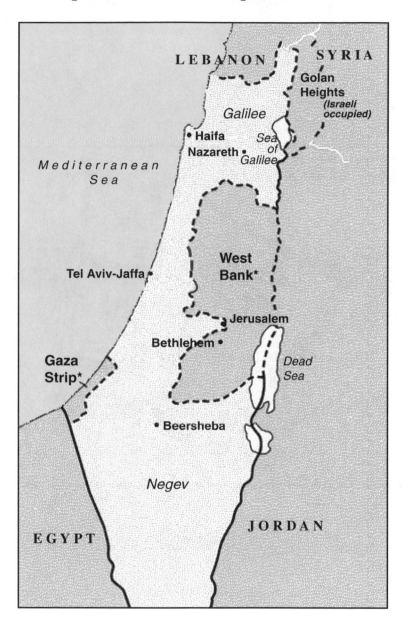

* Israeli occupied with current status subject to the Israeli-Palestinian Interim Agreement—permanent status to be determined through further negotiation.

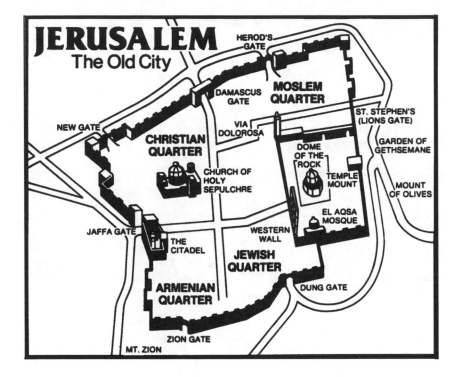

JERUSALEM
The Old City

HEROD'S GATE

DAMASCUS GATE

MOSLEM QUARTER

NEW GATE

VIA DOLOROSA

ST. STEPHEN'S (LIONS GATE)

CHRISTIAN QUARTER

DOME OF THE ROCK

GARDEN OF GETHSEMANE

CHURCH OF HOLY SEPULCHRE

TEMPLE MOUNT

MOUNT OF OLIVES

EL AQSA MOSQUE

JAFFA GATE

THE CITADEL

WESTERN WALL

JEWISH QUARTER

DUNG GATE

ARMENIAN QUARTER

ZION GATE

MT. ZION

26

THE WALLS AND GATES OF JERUSALEM

The Walls

The present walls date only from the time of Suleiman the Magnificent in the sixteenth century. In certain places at the base of the walls can be detected the remnants of the walls of earlier ages, even going back to Herod, and perhaps even Solomon. Comparison with the Model of Jerusalem at the Holy Land Hotel shows that the city enclosed by the wall today is much smaller than at the time of Jesus. Mount Zion, the area of St. Peter in Gallicantu and of the Christian cemeteries, and the ancient City of David (the Jerusalem of Melchizedek and Abraham, Gen 14:17-20) were left outside of Suleiman's walls. (Admission to the walk on top of the walls is at Jaffa Gate.)

The Gates

Damascus Gate, an entrance to old Jerusalem

Damascus Gate: The most beautiful of all the gates of Jerusalem, this is where St. Paul would have exited the city on his way to persecute the Christians. Today it faces the beginning of Nablus Road, along which are found the renowned Ecole Biblique et Archaeologique Francaise with its Basilica of St. Stephen and the so-called Garden Tomb. The Arabs call the Gate Bab el Awad (pillar), keeping alive the ancient memory of a pillar that used to be inside it as depicted on the Madaba Map. Walking under the bridge (lovely spot for mint tea!) that joins the gate with the street is the remnant of part of the gate of Hadrian's Aelia Capitolina of A.D. 135. The difference in the levels of the two gates is due to the destruction caused by war. Inside the gate, the two markets follow the paths of the major thoroughfares that the Romans laid out, the Cardo Minimus, paralleling the Temple Mount, and the Cardo Maximus, crossing the city from north to south. On the left is the Moslem quarter, and on the right the Christian quarter. Where the Cardo runs through the Jewish quarter, it has been restored as a major shopping center.

New Gate: Opened in 1887, this gate gives Christians more direct access to their quarter and the heart of it, the basilica that enshrines the places of the dying and rising of the Lord Jesus. Immediately to the left, inside, is the rear entrance to St. Savior's Convent, headquarters of the Franciscan Custody of the Holy Land and the parish church of the Latin rite Catholics of Jerusalem, many of them descendants of the Crusaders. Also located here are the headquarters of the Greek and Latin Patriarchs and those of many other leaders of the Christian rites. Outside the gate, across the street is the St. Louis Hospice and the Vatican's Notre Dame Centre for pilgrims.

Jaffa Gate: What is mistaken to be the gate is actually an opening in the wall alongside the gate, made at the end of the last century to allow the Kaiser to parade into the city on his horse. The Arab name is Bab el Khalil (friend). For a pilgrimage to Khalil (Hebron) to the tomb of Abraham the friend of God would begin from this gate. It is also the gate from which one would set forth for Jaffa (Yaffo) on the coast. Inside, straight ahead is the Suq or David Street. To the left is the entrance to the wall walk. The first street leads to the Latin Patriarchate, and the second one leads to the magnificent church of the Greek Catholic Patriarchate. To the right is the foundation of one of the Herodian towers, later erroneously called David's fortress or citadel. It now houses the fascinating Museum of the City of Jerusalem. Across from its front entrance is the Christian Information Center, a great resource for the bewildered traveler, and where priests can make reservations for Mass at the Holy Places. Outside the Gate, Jaffa Road leads past the City Hall, and into the business and entertainment area of West Jerusalem.

Zion Gate: The road between Jaffa and Zion Gates continues inside the wall at the edge of the Armenian Quarter. It passes between the Cathedral of St. James and the seminary built where the palace of Herod used to stand. The "design" made by the guns and mortars on the wall outside the Zion Gate is testimony to the flight of the Jews in 1948 and their return in 1967. Outside the Gate, on Mount Zion, are the Franciscan Chapel of the Cenacle (door marked by Holy Land Cross), the Cenacle above the so-called "tomb of David" and the Dormition Abbey. Below the parking lot and across the road is the Church of St. Peter in Gallicantu (where the cock crowed) and the Latin parish cemetery.

Dung Gate: Inside the wall along the edge of the Jewish quarter the road leads to the gate which was once just an aperture for emptying the chamber pots. Today it leads into the Western Wall, and the ramp to the Dome of the Rock on the Haram esh Sharif, the Holy Places of Judaism and Islam. Above are the new or restored buildings of the Jewish quarter, reconstructed after 1967. Outside the gate the road leads down to ancient Jerusalem, today the Arab village of Silwan (Siloam) with its excavations of the City of David.

Golden Gate: Visible from the Kidron Valley and the Mount of Olives, this sealed-up gate may be the beautiful gate of Acts 3. Its predecessor in the time of Jesus was probably the witness to the Palm Sunday procession. Legend has it that it will be opened only for the solemn entrance of the Messiah. Another legend has it that the Moslems have put their graves in front of it to prevent his coming since he would be rendered unclean by passing over corpses. Another legend has it that the rabbis declared that it is only walking over the corpses of Jews that would defile him.

St. Stephen's Gate: Known also as Lions' Gate or Jordan Gate, leads from the Kidron valley with its Church of St. Stephen, Church of all Nations, and the tomb of Mary. Inside on the left are the entrances (for Moslems only) to what Jews call the Temple Mount, and Moslems call the Haram esh Sharif or Noble Sanctuary. Straight ahead begins the Via Dolorosa. The second entrance to the right leads into the Pool of Bethsaida and the Crusader Church of St. Ann, which a late tradition identifies as the birthplace of Mary.

Herod's Gate: Near the Rockefeller Museum and at the beginning of the main street (Saladin or Salah ed Din) of East Jerusalem, this gate leads into the Moslem quarter. Following either alley inside will lead to the Via Dolorosa.

Psalm 122:1-3, 6-8

I rejoiced when they said to me
"Let us go to the House of the Lord."
And now our feet are standing
within your gates, O Jerusalem.
Jerusalem, built as a city
walled round about.
For the peace of Jerusalem pray:
May those who love you prosper!
May peace be within your ramparts,
prosperity within your towers.
For family and friends I say,
"May peace be yours."

JERUSALEM'S HOLY PLACES

The Pool of Bethsaida

Inside St. Stephen's gate the northern portal of the Temple Mount appears on the left, and the second entrance on the right opens onto the property of the White Fathers of Africa founded by Cardinal Lavigerie (bust in the quadrangle) for the evangelization of the African peoples. Since their culture is more akin to Eastern than Western Christianity, he established here a seminary for the clergy of the Eastern, Melkite, or Greek Catholic rite (their Patriarchal Vicar resides inside Jaffa Gate).

Excavations have revealed the pool with five porticoes of John 5. Take that on faith (not in God but the archaeologists!). The site has many layers, and is confusing even with the fine explanatory signs. Long before the pool was sacred to the Christians or Jews, it was one of the healing places dedicated to the god Serapis (Greek: Aesclepius) which are found throughout the Mediterranean. The very name Beth Saida means House of Healing. Those who are constantly searching for hidden symbolism in John's Gospel were amazed to learn John's pool with five porticoes was shown by the archaeologists to be a pool with five porticoes.

John 5:2-18

In Jerusalem, not far from the "Sheep Gate" there is a pool with
five porticoes, called Bethesda. Among the many disabled who lay

there was one man who had been crippled for thirty-eight years. Jesus caught sight of him and was aware of his condition. He asked him if he wanted his health back. The man replied that he was frustrated when the water of the pool was stirred up since someone else always got in the water ahead of him. Jesus said: "Rise, pick up your mat, and walk." And that is exactly what he did!

Keep in mind that this all happened on a sabbath. The guardians of the law let him know in no uncertain terms that he was a sabbath breaker. His defense was that the very one who had healed him had also told him to pick up his mat and walk.

They countered, "And who might that be?" But even though he had his health back, the man was not able to identify who it was that had made him well, since Jesus had slipped through the crowd. Later, however, Jesus caught sight of him and warned him: "You are healthy now, so avoid sinning, or you may find yourself worse off than you were." The man went and told the religious leaders that it was Jesus who had restored him to health. This gave them the opportunity to start attacking Jesus as a sabbath breaker. But he had an answer for them: "Since my Father works on the sabbath, so do I." That was it! They began their plot against his life, since he was not only a sabbath breaker, but a blasphemer who claimed he was equal to God.

NOTE: In the Gospel account, the opponents of Jesus would be correct in the accusation of blasphemy, except that he *is* the Son of God. He uses against them the rabbinical argument that God must work even on the sabbath to sustain his creation. Otherwise it would revert into the chaos from which he brought it. As the Son, Jesus does the same by his healing on the sabbath.

Reflection

Suffering can diminish people or make them grow. How sad it is to encounter those who have become whiners or complainers when faced with the burden of illness or age. What a joy to come in contact with those whose spirit glows even because of suffering. What accounts for the difference? Some ask the right question, and some ask the wrong question.

Some ask, Why is God doing this to me, or What did I do to deserve this? That is the wrong question, but even Jesus' disciples asked it. "Rabbi, who sinned, this man or his parents, that he should be born blind?" (John 9:2) The question presumes that all suffering is due to personal sin and comes as a punishment from a vindictive God. It has been called "ambush" theology. It presents an angry and mean-spirited God who is just waiting for us to make a false move. Hardly the image of his Father that Jesus gives us.

Such a question is fundamentally wrong because it has no answer. It can only lead to frustration or even loss of faith. Even Jesus did not tell us why there is suffering in the world or where it comes from. Instead, he helped us to ask the right question. "What can I do with this illness, this suffering?" This question has an answer that will enable us to grow and to help others. We can do with our suffering what Jesus did with his. We can embrace it with love and join in his saving work. Because we are one with him, he is willing to make our sufferings his own.

Jesus did not physically cure everyone he met, as he cured this man at the pool. He does not say to everyone, "Rise and walk." But he is always willing to heal. He may begin the healing by helping us to ask the right question.

Prayer

Father, help us to realize that suffering has taken on a whole new dimension since your Son embraced the cross near here. Pour out your blessing on all who continue the ministry of Jesus in the healing professions. (NAMES) . . . . Touch those burdened with the cross of illness. (NAMES) . . . . And to all of us give a heart filled with love so that the evil of suffering may be transformed into the glory of Jesus' sacrifice. We ask this through Christ, Our Lord.

> If the group has a priest, the anointing of the sick may be administered so that the healing touch of Jesus may vividly be felt in this place once again. Or, the leader or members of the group may sign each other with the cross on the forehead, saying:

By his holy cross and by the prayer of his Church, may the Lord Jesus, who cured the sick in this holy place grant you fullness of life and health of mind and body.

Church of St. Ann

The inscription over the portal gives a clue as to how this Crusader Church survived so well for almost a thousand years. Saladin, who defeated the Crusaders in 1187, established a school for the study of the Koran here. The Crusaders had built it in honor of St. Ann, Jesus' grandmother, believing that his mother, Mary, was born here. The place of her nativity is celebrated in the crypt, and is beautifully commemorated in the striking icon in the niche on the way back up.

Prayer for Grandparents and Their Grandchildren

That God may bless all grandparents and give them joy in their grand-children, let us pray to the Lord. **Lord, hear our prayer.**

For the grandparents among us, especially those who have the brightest, most clever, and most handsome grandchildren, let us pray to the Lord . . .

That Sts. Joachim and Ann may obtain God's protection and blessing on the grandchildren of our pilgrims, let us pray to the Lord . . .

For those of our grandparents who have joined Joachim and Ann, their daughter Mary, and their grandson, Jesus in the heavenly Jerusalem, let us pray to the Lord . . .

Hail Mary, Full of Grace . . . .

Hymn: *Hail Mary, Gentle Woman* (page 160)

The Via Dolorosa

Via Dolorosa, or Way of the Cross, old city

The soldiers of the Israel Defense Forces (IDF) that may be visible near the first station are not there as stage props. They are guarding the exit to the controversial tunnel dug from the Western Wall plaza to the Fortress Antonia. History repeats itself. Herod had built the Fortress overlooking the Temple Mount so that the Roman Garrison could look on the sacred precinct and preserve the peace.

The present Via Dolorosa presumes that Jesus' trial before Pilot took place here. Each Friday afternoon the Franciscans of the Custody of the Holy Land lead a public procession following this route. Some scholars hold that the trial took place at Herod's palace, south of the Jaffa Gate across from the Cathedral of St. James, at the entrance to the Armenian quarter. Then the historical route would go to the Jaffa Gate, down the suq of David Street, near the present day Lutheran church, and out the gate of the city near the Alexander Hospice. However, it should not be forgotten that when Jesus said: "You cannot be my disciple unless you take up your cross and follow me," he was not referring to the alleys or pathways of Jerusalem. The historical route is not of paramount importance; the following of Jesus is.

What is not disputed is that the ancestors of today's cajoling, persistent merchants had no more interest in the sufferings of Jesus than their descendants have in your piety. Nor, then as now, did the shoppers and pressing crowds have your prayerful spirit as their first priority. You will be making the stations, not like you have made them in your church, but in the streets of Jerusalem, just as Jesus did.

The following suggested meditations have been composed with two things in mind: 1) Where there is no biblical support for the stations, e.g., the falls, and/or 2) where the location does not offer the opportunity for prayerful reflection, the suggested prayers will be shorter.

Each station is begun with:

℣. *We adore you, most Holy Lord, Jesus Christ, and we bless you.*
℟. *Because by your Holy Cross you have redeemed the world.*

FIRST STATION

The Franciscan Biblical School, with its pleasant courtyard and chapels of the condemnation and the carrying of the cross, offers a prayerful atmosphere to begin the stations. If the press of pilgrims is not too heavy, the second station may be prayed in the excavations of the *Ecce Homo* convent next door. The ancient street whose stones are visible in the rear of the Franciscan Chapel continues at the far end of the excavations at Ecce Homo.

Jesus is condemned to death

℣. *We adore you, most Holy Lord, Jesus Christ, and we bless you.*
℟. *Because by your Holy Cross you have redeemed the world.*

John 19:1-11

Narrator: Then Pilate took Jesus and had him scourged. And the soldiers wove a crown out of thorns and placed it on his head, and clothed him in a purple cloak and they came to him and said,

Mob: "Hail, King of the Jews!"

Narrator: And they struck him repeatedly. Once more Pilate went out and said to them,

Pilate: "Look, I am bringing him out to you, so that you may know that I find no guilt in him."

Narrator: So Jesus came out, wearing the crown of thorns and the purple cloak, and Pilate said to them,

Pilate: "Behold the Man" (Latin: *Ecce Homo*).

Narrator: When the chief priests and the guards saw him they cried out,

Mob: "Crucify him, crucify him!"

Pilate: "Take him yourselves and crucify him. I find no guilt in him."

Mob: "We have a law and according to that law he ought to die, because he made himself the Son of God."

Narrator: Now when Pilate heard this statement, he became even more afraid, and went back into the praetorium and said to Jesus,

Pilate: "Where are you from?"

Narrator: Jesus did not answer him.

Pilate: "Do you not speak to me? Do you not know that I have power to release you and I have power to crucify you?"

Jesus: "You would have no power over me if it had not been given to you from above. For this reason the one who handed me over to you has the greater sin."

Narrator: Consequently, Pilate tried to release him but the mob cried out:

Mob: "If you release him, you are no 'Friend of Caesar.' Everyone who makes himself a king opposes Caesar."

Prayer

Lord Jesus, ours is the guilt, yours is the judgment, ours is the crime, yours is the punishment. Forgive us for we knew not what we did. Foolish and stubborn, yet we are the sheep you came to save. Good Shepherd, we

follow your sorrowful way this day, praying that you may lead us in all your ways. Amen.

Hymn:

3. And when I think that God, His Son not sparing,
   Sent Him to die, I scarce can take it in
   That on the cross, my burden gladly bearing,
   He bled and died to take away my sin!

   Refrain:
   Then sings my soul, my Savior God, to Thee;
   How great Thou art, how great Thou art!
   Then sings my soul, my Savior God, to Thee;
   How great Thou art, how great Thou art!

SECOND STATION

Approaching the Ecce Homo Convent, notice the arch across the Via Dolorosa before entering. Once thought to be where Pilate stood when he proclaimed "Behold the Man" *(Ecce Homo),* it is now known to be the center of the triumphal arch at the entrance of the forum of Hadrian's Aelia Capitolina a century after the trial of Jesus. However, the games of the soldiers scratched upon the paving stones in the crypt could well be from Jesus' time. Brochures available at the desk contain information on the Sisters of Zion, the site, and their programs of continuing education.

Jesus embraces the cross

℣. *We adore you, most Holy Lord, Jesus Christ, and we bless you.*
℟. *Because by your Holy Cross, you have redeemed the world.*

John 19:12-17

> **Narrator:** Pilate brought Jesus out and he sat down on the judgment seat in the place called Stone Pavement, *Gabbatha* in Hebrew. It was preparation day for Passover, and it was about noon.
>
> **Pilate:** "Behold your King!"
>
> **Mob:** "Take him away, take him away. Crucify him, crucify him!"
>
> **Pilate:** "Shall I crucify your king?"
>
> **Mob:** "Caesar is our king, we have no other."
>
> **Narrator:** Then Pilate handed Jesus over to the mob to be crucified. So they took Jesus, carrying the cross himself, out to the place called Skull Hill, *Golgotha* in Hebrew.

Prayer

Lord Jesus, no power in heaven or on earth forced you. With love you stretched out your arms to embrace the cross. From a witness to death, the cross became a herald of life. Come and lift up our sagging arms. Make our way of the cross your own and fill our hearts with your love. Amen.

Hymn:

Crown him with many crowns,
The Lamb upon his throne;
Hark! How the heav'nly anthem drowns
All music but its own.
Awake, my soul, and sing
Of him who set us free,
And hail him as your heav'nly King
Through all eternity.

THIRD STATION

At the next corner, the courtyard of the Armenian Catholic Church provides a sheltered spot for the third and fourth stations.

Jesus falls the first time

℣. *We adore you, most Holy Lord, Jesus Christ, and we bless you.*
℟. *Because by your Holy Cross, you have redeemed the world.*

Colossians 1:13-20

Narrator: (The Father) delivered us from the power of darkness and transferred us to the kingdom of his beloved Son, in whom we have redemption, the forgiveness of sins.

All: He is the image of the invisible God, the firstborn of all creation.

Narrator: For in him were created all things in heaven and on earth, the visible and the invisible, whether thrones or dominations or principalities or powers.

All: All things were created through him and for him.

Narrator: He is before all things, and in him all things hold together. He is the head of the Body which is the Church. He is the beginning; he is the firstborn from the dead.

All: He is the image of the invisible God, the firstborn of all creation.

Narrator: He is the beginning, he is the firstborn from the dead. In him all the fullness of divinity dwells. And God was pleased to reconcile all things through him. In him he made peace by the blood of his cross.

All: All things were created through him and for him, for he is the image of the invisible God, the firstborn of all creation.

Prayer

Jesus, you came to this world not as a stranger. You came to embrace us as your brothers and sisters. You are the heartbeat of this world; you are the center of gravity of this universe. Lift us up and restore us with your amazing grace. Without you we will fall again and again and again. Amen.

Hymn:

1. Amazing grace! how sweet the sound,
   That saved a soul like me!
   I once was lost, but now am found,
   Was blind, but now I see.

FOURTH STATION

Jesus meets his mother, Mary

℣. *We adore you, most Holy Lord, Jesus Christ, and we bless you.*
℟. *Because by your Holy Cross, you have redeemed the world.*

Luke 2:34-35

Simeon blessed them and said to Mary, his mother, "Behold this child is destined for the fall and rise of many in Israel, and to be a sign that will be contradicted and a sword will pierce your heart."

John 19:26-27

Standing by the cross of Jesus were his mother, and his mother's sister, Mary the wife of Clopas, and Mary Magdalene. When Jesus saw his mother, and the disciple whom he loved, he said to his mother, "Woman, behold your son." Then he said to the disciple: "Behold your mother." And from that hour, the disciple took her into his home.

Prayer

Jesus, from the cross you gave us your mother to be our own. From first to last she shows us how to be your disciples. "Be it done unto me according to your word" is ever on her lips. May it also be on ours. Amen.

Hymn:

1. At the cross her station keeping,
   Mary stood in sorrow, weeping,
   When her son was crucified.

FIFTH STATION

Simon from Cyrene helps Jesus

℣. *We adore you, most Holy Lord, Jesus Christ, and we bless you.*
℟. *Because by your Holy Cross, you have redeemed the world.*

Luke 23:26

> As they led him away they took hold of a certain Simon, a Cyrenian, who was coming in from the country; and after laying the cross on him, they made him carry it behind Jesus.

Prayer

God, bless the Simons of this world. They meet the weak and they provide strength. They see the fallen and they lift them up. They are disturbed by injustice and they do something. They live the gospel and don't just mouth it. Shake us up that we may be counted among them. Amen.

Hymn:

Refrain:
Whatsoever you do to the least of my people,
that you do unto me.

When I was weary, you helped me find rest;
When I was anxious, you calmed all my fears.
Now enter into the home of my Father.

SIXTH STATION

If the Little Sister of Jesus [cf. Nazareth, Chas. de Foucald] is in the shop next door she will generally allow access to the lovely little chapel at this station. The station is derived from two sources: 1) Veronica personifies the women mentioned in the gospel who ministered to Jesus, and 2) her name, Veronica, is taken from the Greek word for true image *(veron icon).*

Veronica wipes the face of Jesus

℣. *We adore you, most Holy Lord, Jesus Christ, and we bless you.*
℟. *Because by your Holy Cross, you have redeemed the world.*

2 Corinthians 4:5

> We do not proclaim ourselves; we proclaim Jesus Christ as Lord.
> . . . For it is God who said, "Let light shine out of darkness," who
> has shown in our hearts to give the light of the knowledge of the glory
> of God in the face of Jesus Christ.

Prayer

How busy and preoccupied were those who passed you by, Jesus. They could spare an hour for God on the Sabbath but for the rest of the time they had to be careful. Their neighbors might think they were religious fanatics. The next time we rush past you, bring us to our knees. Open our eyes to see that the face is yours. Amen.

Hymn:

Refrain:
Whatsoever you do to the least of my people,
that you do unto me.

You saw me covered with spittle and blood;
You knew my features, though grimy with sweat.
Now enter into the home of my Father.

SEVENTH STATION

This is at the busiest intersection in the Old City. It is better to pray in the chapel of the previous station or up Aqabat el Khanga, a bit near the next station.

Jesus falls the second time

℣. *We adore you, most Holy Lord, Jesus Christ, and we bless you.*
℟. *Because by your Holy Cross, you have redeemed the world.*

Ephesians 1:3-10

> **All:** Blessed be the God and Father of Our Lord Jesus Christ.

> **Narrator:** He has blessed us in Christ with every spiritual blessing in the heavens. He chose us in him before the foundation of the world, that we might be holy and spotless before him.

> **All:** Blessed be the God and Father of our Lord Jesus Christ.

> **Narrator:** In love he destined us for adoption to himself through Jesus Christ . . . In him we have redemption by his blood, the forgiveness of transgressions in accord with the riches of his grace that he lavished upon us.

> **All:** Blessed be the God and Father of our Lord Jesus Christ.

Prayer

"Was it not necessary that the Messiah should suffer these things and thus enter into his glory?"

Yes, Jesus, but that is so difficult to remember when our legs are pulled out from under us. But you were there before us. Strengthen us in our weakness; raise us when we fall. Amen.

Hymn:

Refrain:
Yes, I shall arise and return to my Father!

3. My heart and soul shall yearn for your face;
   Be gracious to me and answer my plea.

EIGHTH STATION

Rather than turning left into the suq (market) toward the Holy Sepulcher, for this station one must go a little way up the Aqabat el Khanga to the cross on the wall on the left. However, if you are more concerned with prayer than with geographical authenticity, then proceed left along the Suq until you reach a staircase on your right. There, calm emerges above the storm and prayer is possible in the quiet of the alley that passes the Coptic monastery and leads to the Ethiopian monastery on the roof of the chapel of St. Helena.

Jesus meets the daughters of Jerusalem

℣. *We adore you, most Holy Lord, Jesus Christ, and we bless you.*
℟. *Because by your Holy Cross, you have redeemed the world.*

Luke 23:27-31

> A large crowd of people followed Jesus, including many women who mourned and lamented him. Jesus turned to them and said, "Daughters of Jerusalem, do not weep for me; weep instead for yourselves and for your children, for indeed, the days are coming when people will say, 'Blessed are the barren, the wombs that never bore and the breasts that never nursed.' At that time, people will say to the mountains, 'Fall upon us!' and to the hills, 'Cover us!' for if these things are done when the wood is green, what will happen when it is dry?"

Prayer

Gentle Savior, in the midst of your torture you allude to violence. The dry wood which is to come will feed the fire of revolt. Violence, revolution and war are no answer. As your disciples, may we be the green wood of life. Through our work for peace and justice, may your kingdom come. For you are our peace. Amen.

Hymn:

Make me a channel of your peace.
Where there is hatred, let me bring your love.
Where there is injury, your pardon, Lord,
And where there's doubt, true faith in you.

NINTH STATION

If you have prayed the previous station where it is marked, then backtrack through the Suq and ascend the stairs to your right. Follow the alley and at the end there is a pillar in the corner. This station may be prayed here or in the chapel of the gracious and ascetic Ethiopian monks. However, it is a place of prayer, and it is ill-mannered simply to use it as a shortcut to the courtyard of the Holy Sepulcher. An offering should be made on the plate in the rear. Otherwise, retrace your steps down the alley and the staircase. Turning right from the Suq, pass the Alexander Hospice of the White Russians where the excavations in the crypt include elements from Constantine's Basilica, Hadrian's Forum, and the gate of the city at the time of Jesus. The entrance to the courtyard of the Basilica of the Holy Sepulcher is straight ahead.

Jesus falls the third time

℣. *We adore you, most Holy Lord, Jesus Christ, and we bless you.*
℞. *Because by your Holy Cross, you have redeemed the world.*

Romans 8:28-39

> **All:** If God is for us who can be against us?
>
> **Narrator:** For those who love God, all things work together unto good. . . . For those he foreknew, he also predestined that they might be conformed to the image of his Son, so that he might be the first born of all.
>
> **All:** If God is for us who can be against us?
>
> **Narrator:** Those he predestined, he also called; those he called, he also justified; those he justified he also glorified.
>
> **All:** If God is for us who can be against us?

Narrator: He who did not spare his own Son, but handed him over for us all, will he not give us everything else along with him? It is Christ Jesus who died and was raised, who is now at God's right hand interceding for us.

All: If God is for us who can be against us?

Narrator: I am convinced that neither death, nor life, nor angels, nor principalities, nor present things, nor future things, nor powers, nor height, nor depth, nor any other creature will be able to separate us from the Love of God which is in Christ Jesus, Our Lord.

All: If God is for us, who can be against us?

Prayer
AMEN! AMEN! AMEN!

Hymn:

Hail, redeemer, king divine!
Priest and lamb, the throne is thine;
King whose reign shall never cease,
Prince of everlasting peace.

Refrain:
Angels, saints and nations sing:
"Praised be Jesus Christ our king;
Lord of earth and sky and sea,
King of love on Calvary."

TENTH STATION

Inside the door of the Basilica of the Holy Sepulcher (more appropriately called the Anastasis or Resurrection, as the Orthodox do) is a staircase to the top of the fragmented stone hill of Calvary. The tenth and eleventh stations may be prayed at the Latin altar, and the twelfth at the Orthodox altar where one may touch the top of the rock of Calvary. If the crowds are as heavy as usual or the narrow, high steps are a challenge, the "chapel of Adam" where the fissure in the rock of Calvary is visible may provide a prayerful alternative.

Jesus is stripped of his garments

℣. *We adore you, most Holy Lord, Jesus Christ, and we bless you.*
℟. *Because by your Holy Cross, you have redeemed the world.*

John 19:23-24

The soldiers took his clothes and divided them into four shares, one for each soldier. They also took his tunic, but the tunic was seamless, woven in one piece from the top down. So they said to one another, "Let us not tear it, but cast lots for it to determine who will get it." This happened that the Scripture might be fulfilled: "They divided my garments among them, and for my vesture they cast lots."

Prayer

Jesus, although you were God, you were not miserly about your divine prerogatives. For our sakes you made yourself poor, you emptied yourself, and your Father exalted you as Lord. Empty us of self. Be Lord of our lives. Amen.

Hymn:

2. If you pass through raging waters in the sea, you shall not drown.
   If you walk amid the burning flames, you shall not be harmed.
   If you stand before the power of hell and death is at your side,
   Know that I am with you through it all.

Refrain:
Be not afraid; I go before you always.
Come, follow me, and I will give you rest.

ELEVENTH STATION

The top of Calvary, unlike the seamless garment of Jesus, is divided. The mosaic of the nailing to the cross with the adjoining altar of Our Lady of Sorrows is Latin, while the newly restored sanctuary of the Crucifixion is Greek Orthodox.

Jesus is nailed to the cross

℣. *We adore you, most Holy Lord, Jesus Christ, and we bless you.*
℟. *Because by your Holy Cross, you have redeemed the world.*

John 19:18-22

They crucified him, and with him two others, one on either side, with Jesus in the middle. Pilate also had an inscription written and put on the cross. It read: "Jesus of Nazareth, the King of the Jews."

Prayer

Jesus, nails did not hold you to the cross; love did. You did not just say, "Greater love than this has no one than that they give their life for their friends." You did it! You did it for me! Thank you, thank you, thank you. Amen.

Hymn:

Were you there when they crucified my Lord?
Were you there when they crucified my Lord?

O! Sometimes it causes me to tremble, tremble, tremble.
Were you there when they crucified my Lord?

TWELFTH STATION

Jesus dies upon the cross

℣. *We adore you, most Holy Lord, Jesus Christ, and we bless you.*
℟. *Because by your Holy Cross, you have redeemed the world.*

John 19:28-30

> After this, aware that everything was now finished in order that the
> scripture might be fulfilled, Jesus said, "I thirst." There was a container
> of common wine nearby. So they put a sponge soaked in wine on a sprig
> of hyssop and held it up to his mouth. When Jesus had taken the wine,
> he said, "It is finished." And bowing his head, he handed over the Spirit.

Prayer in Silence

Hymn:

Refrain:
Let all that is within me cry holy;
Let all that is within me cry holy.

Holy, holy, holy is the Lamb that was slain. *(Refrain)*
Glory to the Lamb that was slain. *(Refrain)*
Jesus is the Lamb that was slain. *(Refrain)*

THIRTEENTH STATION

The red stone marking the place of the preparation of the body of Jesus
for burial was placed there only in the last century. The beautiful new mosaic on the wall behind it vividly tells the story of the descent from the
cross, the preparation for burial and the entombment.

The body of Jesus is taken down and prepared for burial

℣. *We adore you, most Holy Lord, Jesus Christ, and we bless you.*
℟. *Because by your Holy Cross, you have redeemed the world.*

John 19:38-42

> After this, Joseph of Arimathea, secretly a disciple of Jesus for fear
> of the Jews, asked Pilate if he could remove the body of Jesus. And Pi-
> late permitted it. So he came and took his body. Nicodemus, the one
> who had first come to him at night, also came bringing a mixture of
> myrrh and aloes weighing about one hundred pounds. They took the
> body of Jesus and bound it with burial cloths along with the spices,

according to the Jewish burial custom. Now in the place where he had been crucified there was a garden, and in the garden a new tomb, in which no one had yet been buried. So they laid Jesus there because of the Jewish preparation day; for the tomb was close by.

Prayer

We remember your words, Lord Jesus: "You will grieve for a time, but your grief will turn into joy. I shall see you again, and then your hearts will rejoice, with a joy no one can take from you." This joy is the source of our hope, for the light came into the darkness, and the darkness was not able to overpower it. Amen.

Hymn:

3. Were you there when they laid him in the tomb?
   Were you there when they laid him in the tomb?
   O! Sometimes it causes me to tremble, tremble, tremble.
   Were you there when they laid him in the tomb?

FOURTEENTH STATION

The glory of the newly refurbished dome raises hope that the unsightly nineteenth-century aedicule hiding what remains of the tomb of Jesus may soon achieve the fate that it richly deserves. When Helena built the original rotunda over the grave, she had to cut away the wall of the quarry in which the tomb was a hole. All that is left is the shelf that was in the cave, where Jesus' body was placed. It is now hidden under the altar in the second chamber. In the rear, the Coptic monk invites the credulous to come in and touch it.

If there is a large crowd, space may be found in the "Syrian" chapel with its "tomb of Joseph of Arimathea." Another area is in the Latin section by the choir loft, near the altar of Mary Magdalene, with its bronze bas relief by the late Father Andrea Martini, O.F.M. If it is not in use, the chapel of the Blessed Sacrament is an oasis. Notice the bronze stations by Father Martini, with the Resurrection as the fifteenth.

Jesus is buried and rises to life

℣. *We adore you, most Holy Lord, Jesus Christ, and we bless you.*
℟. *Because by your Holy Cross, you have redeemed the world.*

John 20:11-18

Mary stayed outside the tomb weeping. And as she wept, she bent over into the tomb and saw two angels in white sitting there, one at the head and one at the feet where the body of Jesus had been. They said to her, "Woman, why are you weeping?" She said to them, "They have taken my Lord, and I don't know where they laid him." When she had said this, she turned around and saw Jesus there, but she did not know it was Jesus. Jesus said to her, "Woman, why are you weeping?" She thought it was the gardener and said to him: "Sir, if you carried him away, tell me where you laid him, and I will take him." Jesus said to her, "Mary!" She turned and said to him, "Rabbouni." Jesus said to her, "Stop holding on to me, for I have not yet ascended to the Father. But go to my brothers and tell them, 'I am going to my Father and your Father, to my God and your God.'" Mary Magdalene went and announced to the disciples, "I have seen the Lord."

Prayer

Lord of life, we are Easter Christians and Alleluia is our song! Through the transforming power of your paschal sacrifice, you are the lamb once slain who lives forever. You are our eternal high priest, interceding for us with the Father. May the light of your resurrection shine through us. May we proclaim it by every word and deed: Christ is risen! He is truly risen! Alleluia! Alleluia!

Hymn:

3. I am the Resurrection,
   I am the life.
   If you believe in me,
   Even though you die,
   You shall live forever.

   Refrain:
   And I will raise you up,
   And I will raise you up,
   And I will raise you up on the last day.

The Holy Sepulcher

A.D. 28–29: Outside the Ephraim Gate in the second wall of Jerusalem there is an unused quarry. It is no longer worked because earthquakes have fragmented the stone, especially that in the center which forms a small hill resembling a skull

(Latin: *calvarius*). The Roman authorities used it for capital punishment since it sits alongside a major thoroughfare into the city. Here Jesus was crucified and then buried in a cave in the side of the quarry.

A.D. 40–44: Herod Agrippa builds the third wall enclosing the quarry with the Holy Places of the death and burial of Jesus inside the city.

A.D. 66–70: The first Jewish revolt led by the Zealots is suppressed by Vespasian in Galilee. His troops elect him emperor, and his son and successor Titus destroys the Holy City. The "Burned House" in the Jewish quarter, along with the Sadducee Villa of the Wohl Museum bear testimony to the ferocity of the attack.

A.D. 132–135: The Emperor Hadrian plans to rebuild the city as the capital of the Roman province of Syria Palestina. Named Aelia after his family and Capitolina after the god of Rome, Capitoline Jupiter. The plan enrages the Jews. Shimeon bar Cochba leads the second revolt and establishes the short-lived Jewish state. After the revolt has been suppressed Hadrian continues with his plan to build Aelia Capitolina. He fills in the quarry and builds a Roman Forum upon the rubble with a temple to Jupiter over Calvary. Jews are forbidden to enter the Holy City.

A.D. 325: Having moved the capital of the empire from Rome to Byzantium, Constantine and his mother Helena wipe out the pagan structures and make it a Holy City again by building monuments on Calvary and the Holy Sepulcher. To accomplish the latter, they cut away the quarry, making the tomb disappear, and leaving only the shelf upon which the body of Jesus lay.

A.D. 614: Destroyed by the Persians, the Basilica is soon rebuilt by the Byzantines.

A.D. 638: The Caliph Omar is invited by the Patriarch to pray in the Holy Sepulcher. He declines for fear his followers would then make it into a mosque. He prayed outside, where the Mosque of Omar stands today.

A.D. 1009: The "mad caliph" Hakim leads the persecution of the Christians and the destruction of the shrines.

A.D. 1099:   The Crusaders arrive, establishing the Latin Kingdom of Jerusalem and rebuilding the Holy Sepulcher which is basically the building still in use today. The Crusader Kingdom ends in 1187 with the victory of the Moslems under Saladin.

A.D. 1219:   Francis of Assisi visits the Holy Land and shortly thereafter his followers, the Friars Minor, are established there. They fill the vacuum left by the military crusader monks who were expelled. In 1309 Sultan Baybars II issues a formal document giving the right to the "Brothers of the Cord" to reside at the cenacle on Mount Zion, the Holy Sepulcher and Bethlehem. In 1342 the de facto presence of the Franciscans is recognized by the Holy See and they are made the official guardians of the Holy Places, known as the Custody of the Holy Land.

A.D. 1517:   The Ottoman Turks capture Jerusalem and Suleiman the Magnificent rebuilds the walls that stand today.

A.D. 1848:   In the middle of the nineteenth century the sultan quiets the squabbling among the Christian factions by establishing the "status quo" confirming whatever rights each community was in possession of over the Holy Places at that time. And just to make sure it sticks, the key to the door of the Holy Sepulcher is entrusted to a Moslem family who jealously guard their right to open and close it to this day. At the same time, the Latin Patriarchate is reestablished in Jerusalem with the Holy Sepulcher as the co-cathedral.

A.D. 1917:   The Ottoman Empire is dissolved by the League of Nations and Jerusalem becomes the capital of the British Mandate over Palestine. The Holy Sepulcher is in great danger of collapse due to fires and earthquakes. The bribes *(bakshish)* demanded by the Turks have hindered repairs, and the jealousy of the religious groups has paralyzed the effort.

A.D. 1959:   An international architectural commission, including the famous Br. Cajetan Bauman, O.F.M., of New York, opts for renovation rather than demolition and the work continues with the completion of the dome over the Holy Sepulcher in 1997.

Visit

Holy Sepulchre Church, Jerusalem

The best time to get a few minutes of prayerful peace and quiet is while the horde of tourists are at their hotels having breakfast or supper. Then the only thing to distract from the sacred mystery of Jesus' sacrifice may be the candle vendors on Calvary and within the aedicule of the sepulcher. Even they may illustrate the gospel: Jesus expelled the buyers and sellers from the temple. It is not uncommon here or at other shrines to see an arsenal of weapons near the entrance, with a young soldier watching over them. The recruits of the Israeli Defense Forces routinely go on tours, even of the Christian shrines, and they are not permitted to take their guns inside.

Outside the entrance is the staircase to the crusader chapel adjacent to Calvary, accessible only for those with reservations for Mass. Immediately to the right, inside the door, is one of two steep staircases giving access to Calvary itself. On the top, either in front of the Latin altar of the nailing to the cross, the bejewelled shrine of the Sorrowful Mother, or the Greek altar above the summit of Calvary, now visible through the glass, it is permitted for groups to pray aloud or sing if there is no ceremony in progress. However, it may be best to stand or kneel in awe.

John 3:14-16; 10:17-18; 15:12-13; 19:26-30

> Just as Moses lifted up the serpent in the desert, so must the Son of Man be lifted up, so that everyone who believes in him may have eternal life, for God so loved the world that he offered his only Son, so that everyone who believes in him might not perish but might have

eternal life, for God did not send his Son into the world to condemn the world, but that the world might be saved through him. This is why the Father loves me, because I myself lay down my life in order to take it up again. No one takes it from me, but I lay it down on my own. This is my commandment: love one another as I have loved you. No one has greater love than this: to lay down one's life for one's friends. **And bowing his head, he handed over the spirit.**

Chapel of Adam

Beneath Calvary the cracked stone is visible behind the glass in the chapel of Adam. The skull and cross bones beneath the feet of Jesus on some crucifixes are a reminder of the medieval legend that Adam was buried at the base of Calvary.

Romans 5:15

But the gift is all out of proportion to the offense. For if by Adam's offense the many died, how much more did the grace of God and the gracious gifts of the one person, Jesus Christ, abound for the many.

Stone of Anointing

While the local populace retained the authentic memories of the places of Jesus' death and resurrection, curious pilgrims sought to identify the location of every detail. And the local populace was reluctant to say "We don't know." Thus the red marble slab placed here in the nineteenth century purportedly marks the place where Jesus' body was prepared for burial, as the cage-like structure by the staircase of the Armenians supposedly marks where the women stood at a distance.

The Tomb

It is encouraging that the early Christian faithful retained the memory of the place where their Savior was buried. What can be discouraging is the unsightly aedicule raised over it in the last century, the proliferation of icons hanging within and without, the grime from the lamps, the competing candlesticks of each special interest group, and the candle concession within. Fortunately our faith is in the Risen Lord and not in the empty tomb.

1 Corinthians 15:1-4

I am reminding you of the gospel I preached to you . . . through it you are also being saved if you hold fast to the word I preached to you . . . for I handed on to you as of primary importance what I also

> received: that Christ died for our sins in accordance with the scrip-
> tures; that he was buried; that he was raised on the third day in accor-
> dance with the scriptures.

In front of the tomb, the nave of the church has been blocked off with
the walls erected between the pillars, and has become the *Catholicon* of
the Greek Orthodox.

The Roman Catholic sanctuary includes the choir loft with its magnificent new organ and the bronze frieze by Fr. Andrea Martini, O.F.M. Opposite is the altar of Mary Magdalene with its bas relief. If you ever
wondered how Mary could have mistaken the risen Jesus for a gardener,
look at the picture under the choir loft where he is depicted with gardener's garb and hoe. A fundamentalist could not have taken the gospel
more literally!

John 20:14-15

> Mary Magdalene turned around and saw Jesus there, but she did
> not know it was Jesus. He said to her, "Woman, why are you weep-
> ing? Whom are you looking for?" She thought it was the gardener
> and said to him, "Sir, if you carried him away, tell me where you laid
> him, and I will take him."

The chapel of the Blessed Sacrament is dedicated to the apparition of
Jesus to his mother. The Gospels make no mention of it, but it is one of the
"mysteries" of the seven joys of the Franciscan rosary, so it must be true! It
is also the choir chapel of the friars who live behind it and are the custodians
of the Holy Sepulcher for the Latin Church. Exiting the Latin area to the left,
one finds an area designated as the "Prison of Christ," apparently because no
one remembered what the area was and curious pilgrims had to know!

Beyond, the chapels which once held the instruments of the passion
(St. Louis IX took the crown of thorns back to Paris and built La Sainte
Chapelle as its reliquary.) is the stairway to the Armenian chapel. Notice
the thousands of crosses carved by your predecessors, the pilgrims over
the centuries. The mosaic in the floor portrays the great churches of Arme-
nia, the first nation to be converted to Christianity. Notice also Mount
Ararat and Noah's Ark. If the custodian is present, it may be possible to
enter through the door on the left side of the sanctuary to view the quarry
and the foundations of the Roman Temple of Hadrian's Aelia Capitolina.
Also to be seen is the extraordinary graffiti made by a very early Christian
pilgrim of a ship, and the words *DOMINE IVIMUS,* reminiscent of Psalm
22, "I rejoiced when they said to me, *we will go* to the house of the *Lord.*"

The stairway at the right descends into the Latin chapel of St. Helena. Clearly part of the quarry, it is thought to have been the cistern where Constantine's mother found the cross of Jesus. The bronze statue depicts her holding it.

Reflection

A visit to this basilica, one of the holiest places in the world, can be disappointing. It is at its worst when various Christian groups are competing for the ear of God. It is like "show and tell," illustrating the tragedy of the divisions in the Church, the Body of Christ. It is contrary to God's will and resulted from narrowmindedness, nationalism, and self-interest. Yet it also shows that the Lord Jesus did not shy from embracing our seared, broken, and scarred humanity. Here he rose from the dead to "free those who through fear of death had been subject to slavery all their life . . . He had to become like (us) in every way, that he might be a merciful and faithful high priest, in order to expiate the sins of the people" (Heb 2:15, 17). Here the power of risen life is offered to all. Here he challenges his disciples to live in such a way that their lives are the best proof that he is risen. ALLELUIA! ALLELUIA! ALLELUIA!

INSIDE THE DIAMOND

City blest-
Diamond
Of heaven
Inside, the
Brilliant
Light is Him

Joan Nancy Vernon Kelly
with permission

Ephesians 1:18-23

May the eyes of your hearts be enlightened that you may know the hope that belongs to his call, what are the riches of glory in his inheritance among the holy ones, and what is the surpassing power of his greatness for us who believe, in accord with the exercise of his great might which he worked in Christ, raising Christ from the dead and seating him at his right hand in the heavens, far above every authority, principality, power and dominion, and every name that is named not only in this age but also in the one to come. And he put all things beneath his feet, and gave him as head over all things to the church, which is his body, the fullness of the one who fills all things in every way.

Hymns: *I Am the Bread of Life* (page 164); *Crown Him with Many Crowns* (page 159); *Alleluia! Sing to Jesus* (page 155); *How Great Thou Art* (vss. 3 and 4; page 163); *Hail, Redeemer, King Divine* (page 161)

A note on the "Garden tomb" or the Protestant Tomb or Gordon's Tomb: On Nablus Road between the Schmitt School and the École Biblique is found the Garden tomb, "discovered" by General Gordon a hundred years ago. No scholar or archaeologist believes that it is the tomb of Jesus. The Holy Sepulcher was outside the walls of Jerusalem in the time of Jesus, which Gordon was unaware of and so set out in hot pursuit of a tomb outside the walls of 1530. In fact, if you could visit the garden of the École Biblique next door, you would be shown far more interesting tombs. The spot, however, is peaceful and prayerful and provides a setting for Protestants to celebrate liturgically the sacrifice and burial of Jesus which actually took place nearby, inside the present walls at the Basilica of the Holy Sepulcher.

St. Stephen's Basilica (École Biblique)

The celebrated Jerusalem Bible, even better in its recent revision, is the fruit of the scholarship of the Dominicans at the École Biblique et Archaeologique Française. Great giants of the biblical movement like Lagrange, de Vaux, Vincent, Benoit, and among the living, Boismard and Murphy-O'Connor engaged in their prophetic work here. It is one of the great power-houses of biblical scholarship. On its grounds (ring the bell at the gate) is the lovely Basilica of St. Stephen. This may commemorate where he was buried in Byzantine times, while the Orthodox Church outside of St. Stephen's Gate may mark the place of his martyrdom.

Acts 7:55–8:2

> Stephen, filled with the Holy Spirit looked up intently to heaven and saw the glory of God and Jesus standing at the right hand of God, and he said, "Behold I see the heavens opened and the Son of Man standing at the right hand of God." But they cried out in a loud voice, covered their ears, and rushed upon him together. They threw him out of the city, and began to stone him. The witnesses laid down their cloaks at the feet of a young man named Saul. As they were stoning Stephen, he called out, "Lord Jesus, receive my spirit." Then he fell to his knees and cried out in a loud voice, "Lord, do not hold this sin against them" and when he said this, he fell asleep. . . . Devout men buried Stephen, and made a loud lament over him.

Mount Zion

Prior to the establishment of the homeland for the Jewish people in 1948, one of the names that was in the running as a title for the new entity was Zion. It was the name given to the movement that brought about the establishment of the new state: Zionism. Obviously, Israel won out, but the name Zion is still dear to God's people.

Although the etymological derivation is unclear, it was already the Canaanite name for Jerusalem when David took it as his capital. "Then David and his men set out for Jerusalem which was inhabited by the Jebusites. . . . He captured the stronghold of Zion, which is the city of David" (2 Sam 5:5, 7). The city referred to is the ridge south of the Temple Mount, now the village of Silwan, outside the present walls, which date from Suleiman the Magnificent in 1530.

The gate in those walls called Zion Gate opens out on the southwestern hill known today as Mount Zion. The holes left by mortars, grenades, and bullets are mute witnesses to the struggle for the control of the "city of peace" in 1948 and 1967.

In the time of Jesus the area was probably an Essene quarter within the ancient walls. Today it contains the Armenian, Orthodox, and Catholic cemeteries (Where the hero of *Schindler's List* is buried). For the pilgrim, it is the site of the Cenacle, the Chapel of the Cenacle, the "tomb of David," and the Dormition Abbey.

The Cenacle Chapel and Upper Room

Exiting the Holy City through Zion Gate, one finds the walled enclosure of the Armenian Patriarchal cemetery. Beyond it, above the parking lot is the doorway, marked by the Holy Land cross which is the entrance to the Chapel of the Cenacle. This compound is a relative newcomer to the area. The Franciscans dwelt here for almost three-hundred years before they were expelled from the property of the actual Cenacle to which they still hold the deed. In the sixteenth century, they and their superior who still retains the title of Guardian of Mount Zion were received by the Armenians until they could obtain the property now used for their headquarters at St. Savior's by the New Gate. The present compound with its bronzes of the Last Supper, the Holy Spirit, and the Virgin by Fr. Andrea Martini in the chapel, its crypt chapel and lovely garden, is a prayerful spot. It is the closest one can get to the site of the Upper Room for the celebration of the liturgy (by reservation only).

The actual Cenacle or Upper Room is located just beyond the Franciscan property where a sign says "House of Prayer for all Nations." Ascend the stairs, pass through the custodian's antechamber and on into the site venerated as the Upper Room. We know that the original was in this area, but is unlikely to have survived the Roman destruction of Jerusalem in A.D. 70. The present room, along with the adjoining Chapel of the Holy Spirit were probably originally part of the huge Byzantine Church of Holy Zion which covered the entire top of this hill. The *mihrab* or prayer niche indicating the direction of Mecca reveals the use to which the room was put after it was seized from the Franciscans in the sixteenth century. However, the capitol of the small pillar at the staircase in the corner testifies to the ancient tradition: the pelican piercing her breast to feed her young is the symbol of the Lord feeding us in the Eucharist!

The Last Supper

Luke 22:10-20

> Jesus sent out Peter and John, and told them: "When you go into the city, a man will meet you carrying a jar of water. Follow him into the house that he enters and say to the master of the house, 'The teacher says to you, "Where is the guest room where I may eat the Passover with my disciples?"'" He will show you a large upper room that is furnished. Make the preparations there." Then they went off and found everything exactly as he had told them, and there they prepared the Passover.
>
> When the hour came, he took his place at table with the apostles. He said to them, "I have eagerly desired to eat this Passover with you before I suffer, for, I tell you, I shall not eat it again until there is fulfillment in the kingdom of God." . . . Then he took the bread, said the blessing, broke it, and gave it to them, saying, "This is my body, which will be given for you; do this in memory of me." And likewise the cup after they had eaten, saying, "This cup is the new covenant in my blood, which will be shed for you."

John 20:19-23

> On the evening of that first day of the week, when the doors were locked, where the disciples were, . . . Jesus came and stood in their midst and said to them, "Peace be with you." When he had said this, he showed them his hands and his side. The disciples rejoiced when they saw the Lord. Jesus said to them again, "Peace be with you. As the Father has sent me, so I send you." And when he had said this, he breathed on them and said to them, "Receive the holy Spirit. Whose sins you forgive are forgiven them, and whose sins you retain are retained."

The sacraments of the Upper Room are Eucharist, confirmation, and the priesthood. While eucharistic liturgy is not permitted here, there seems to be no objection to a less formal ceremony of reading, singing, and anointing to recall the coming of the Holy Spirit. Tracing the sign of the cross on the forehead, say, "REMEMBER THAT YOU ARE THE TEMPLE OF GOD, AND THE HOLY SPIRIT DWELLS IN YOU."

There is no better way to fulfill Jesus' injunction to "do this in memory of me" than with a eucharistic celebration in the Chapel of the Cenacle. The readings for Holy Thursday may be read from the Lectionary. If there are several priests the preface and formula of priestly commitment may be read from the Sacramentary from the Mass for the blessing of the oils. The priests may anoint each other's hands with oil as a reminder of that commitment, with the formula: "May your lives imitate the holiness of the sacred objects that you hold in your hands." The prayer of the faithful may take the form of each member of the group mentioning the names of those priests who have brought them closer to Christ.

Hymns: *Come, Holy Ghost* (page 159); *Like a Shepherd* (page 166); *I Am the Bread of Life* (page 164); *You Satisfy the Hungry Heart* (page 171)

The Tomb of David

The Upper Room is now more accessible than it was when it was a mosque. This is probably due to a misinterpretation of Peter's preaching at Pentecost. Here on Mount Zion he told the crowd that Psalm 16 says that God would not allow his Holy One to see corruption. This obviously, says Peter, cannot refer to David because his tomb is with us to the present day. Peter goes on to show how the Psalmist (David) must have been referring to the Resurrection of the Messiah Jesus. First Kings 2:10 makes very clear that David was buried on the other side of town in the "City of David." A later generation misunderstood Peter to mean that David's tomb was here on Mount Zion, and an unidentified tomb began to be pointed out as his. Because of this "tomb of David" the whole building, including the Cenacle above it, is a national monument of the state of Israel, open to all. Exit the Cenacle, follow the sign and descend, noticing the pillared courtyard which was once the cloistered garden of the Franciscans. The tomb is in a niche that was probably once a part of the Church of Zion. Since the original tomb has been lost, this one provides a fine opportunity to honor David as the ideal Messiah, to whom are attributed so many of those prayers that have nourished our spiritual life.

Psalm 110:1-4

> Yahweh said to my Lord, Come to your throne at my right hand,
> while I subdue your enemies. Yahweh will uphold your authority,
> you will triumph from Zion. In your very birth royal power is yours.
> Like the dew, before the dawn I begot you. Yahweh has sworn and
> he will not reneg on his oath. Yours is an eternal priesthood descended
> from Melchizedek.

Dormition Abbey

The most visible building on Mount Zion is the Benedictine Abbey dedicated to the "sleeping" of Mary. A century ago the Kaiser built for the Lutherans the *Evangelischekirche* near the Holy Sepulcher, and this beautiful Abbey for the Catholics (It is no coincidence that the dome resembles a Prussian soldier's helmet!). The magnificence of the organ, the fine acoustics and the beauty of the mosaic of the Mother and Child *(Theotokos)* make this a splendid setting not only for liturgy, but also for the public concerts that are frequently held here. On the way to the crypt, notice the Christian Zodiac in the floor, a fine example of a flexible Christianity that can baptize even pagan symbols.

The centerpiece of the crypt is the hauntingly beautiful figure of Mary in repose. The mosaic in the baldachino above joins her to the great women of the past: Eve, Miriam, Deborah, Jael, Ruth, and Esther. The Blessed Sacrament Chapel is at the rear, while the ikon facing shows the traditional Byzantine way of depicting the Dormition. Mary is in repose, surrounded by the Apostles, while Jesus is shown with her soul, as the child Mary, in his arms.

1 Corinthians 15:51ff

> Now I can lift the veil for you. We shall not all fall asleep, but we
> will all be changed . . . . For that which is corruptible must clothe it-
> self in incorruptibility and that which is merely flesh must be trans-
> formed into what is immortal. . . . Death is transformed into triumph.
> . . . Let us give thanks to our God who gives us this triumph through
> Jesus Christ who is Lord.

Hymns: *Hail, Holy Queen Enthroned Above* (page 160); *Hail Mary, Gentle Woman* (page 160)

St. Peter in Gallicantu

The church of St. Peter where the cock crowed commemorates Peter's denial at the house of the high priest, as well as Jesus' trial there. It may or may not be the place but the excavations, renewed within recent years, certainly help us to recreate the events in the life of Jesus on the eve of his death. From the observation deck before entering the church, there is an unparalleled view of Haceldema, the City of David, the Mount of Olives, the Kidron Valley, the walls of the city, and the "Pinnacle of the Temple" (southeast corner of the wall).

The church is in the care of the Augustinians of the Assumption (Assumption College, Worcester, Massachusetts). Recent excavation and restoration after a devastating storm have made the site even more beautiful and accessible. Besides the lovely church, the two highlights are the cistern, signed by the crosses of early pilgrims, which may have been used as a prison where Jesus was held overnight, and the stairway to the valley which Jesus would have tread on the way to Gethsemane and return, to stand trial.

In the Cistern

Based on Psalm 88

℞. *Yahweh, my God and my help, hear my prayer.*

℣. *In the darkness of the night, turn toward me. I am burdened beyond measure, my life teeters on the edge of the nether world.*
℞. *Yahweh, my God and my help, hear my prayer.*

℣. *My name is included among those in the pit. I am totally helpless. It is as if I have joined the ranks of the dead, already lowered into the grave.*
℞. *Yahweh, my God and my help, hear my prayer.*

℣. *You have dropped me to the very bottom of the pit. Waves of terror, loneliness and frustration wash over me. My so-called friends have left me in the dust. Where are you? Where are you?*
℞. *Yahweh, my God and my help, hear my prayer.*

Hymn: Yes, I Shall Arise (3X) (page 170)

On the Steps

Matthew 26

> After singing a hymn, they went out to the Mount of Olives. . . . Then all the disciples left him and fled. Those who had arrested Jesus brought him before Caiaphas, the high priest, where the scribes and the elders were assembled. . . . Jesus was silent. Then the high

priest said to him, "I am putting you under oath. Answer me. Are you the Messiah, the Son of God?" Jesus replied: "You have said it, but let me say, **'From now on you will see the Son of Man enthroned at the right hand of the power. He will be coming on the clouds of heaven.'"**

A little later some of the hangers-on tried to point the finger at Peter: "You are one of them; your accent gives you away!" He swore violently in denial. "I do not have anything to do with him." No sooner had he denied that he knew Jesus than the cock crowed.

Hymn: How Great Thou Art (page 163)

Jewish Quarter

After the Six-Day War in 1967 when the Israelis were able once again to enter the Old City, they first allowed the archaeologists in to do their work. Four sites are worth a visit.

1. The Cardo Maximus was originally the great shopping street of Hadrian's Aelia Capitolina, built after the suppression of the second Jewish revolt in A.D. 135. On the wall is a mosaic of the map of Jerusalem, copied from the floor of the sixth-century church at Madaba, Jordan. It is a unique source for the location of buildings in Byzantine Jerusalem, including the Holy Sepulcher midway along the Cardo Maximus.

2. Hezekiah was one of the few great and good messiahs in Judah's history. He was the royal son that the prophet Isaiah had primarily in mind when he challenged the faith of Achaz (Isa 7:14ff). When he succeeded his unfaithful father, the young Hezekiah cleansed Jerusalem and the temple of the idols that had signified submission to Assyria. He was very much aware that he was performing an act of insulting rebellion to his overlord, Sennacherib. Preparing for the certain invasion to follow, he built the wall that is now so beautifully excavated, with a map that clearly explains its significance. At the same time, he dug his water tunnel to frustrate the plans of Sennacherib in 701 B.C. (2 Kings 18, 19). The outcome of the invasion was immortalized by George Gordon, Lord Byron.

The Destruction of Sennacherib

"The Assyrian came down like the wolf on the fold,
and his cohorts were gleaming in purple and gold;

and the sheen of their spears was like stars on the sea.
When the blue wave rolls nightly on deep Galilee.
Like the leaves of the forest when summer is green,
that host with their banners at sunset were seen;
like the leaves of the forest when Autumn hath blown,
that host on the morrow lay withered and strown.
For the angel of death spread his wings on the blast,
and breathed in the face of the foe as he passed;
and the eyes of the sleepers waxed deadly and chill,
and their hearts but once heaved, and forever grew still!
And there lay the steed with his nostrils all wide,
but through it there rolled not the breath of his pride:
And the foam of his gaping lay white on the turf,
and cold as the spray of the rock-beating surf.
And there lay the rider distorted and pale,
with the dew on his brow and rust on his mail.
And the tents were all silent, the banners alone,
the lances unlifted, the trumpet unblown.
And the widows of Ashur are loud in their wail,
and the idols are broke in the temple of Baal;
and the might of the Gentile, unsmote by the sword,
hath melted like snow in the glance of the Lord."

3. The Burned House is a vivid example of the total destruction of Jerusalem by Titus and his legions in A.D. 70. The audience sits overlooking the actual excavation, viewing a multivision slide and audio presentation. The objects found in the excavations (except the female skeletal remains) are well displayed and described. (A joint ticket is available for this and the Sadducee Villa.) Meanwhile, even if you are not hungry, take the staircase right outside the entrance to the Burned House and buy something at the self-service Quarter Cafe, so that you can see the splendid view of the Temple Mount and the Mount of Olives.

4. The Sadducee villas, also destroyed in the conflagration of the year A.D. 70 are extraordinary archaeological displays. The priestly class were reluctant participants in the revolt against the Romans and one can easily see why. They had more to lose.

Western Wall

At the Western Wall, Jerusalem

The wall in question was not part of the Temple. It is part of the retaining wall, originally built by Solomon and expanded by Herod, transforming Mount Moriah into a platform or plateau upon which the Temple was built. It is the most sacred area for the Jews. Near here, in the Holy of Holies of the Temple, it was felt that God dwelled with his people. Menachem Begin is reported to have said to Jimmy Carter, "talking to God from Jerusalem is only a local call." For St. Luke, Jerusalem and the Temple are pivotal in the life and ministry of Jesus. He begins with Zachary offering incense in the Jerusalem Temple; in the Visitation he seems to depict Mary as its new Ark of the Covenant. Jesus is presented in it; as a youth he spends time in it discussing the Torah with the elders; he resists the devil's temptation to leap from its pinnacle; he laments over it; he tells the parable of the Pharisee and the tax collector who prayed there; he cleanses it; he praises the widow who gave her mite to it; and in the next breath foretells its destruction. Then, at his death the curtain of the Temple split down the middle. Still, in his last line, Luke insists that after the Ascension, the first Christians "were continually in the temple praising God."

In John's "replacement theology," Jesus is the new temple: "he was speaking about the temple of his body" (John 2:21). Paul, in trying to help the Christians find a new basis beyond the commandments for their morality and spirituality, insists: ". . . your body is a temple of the Holy Spirit . . . therefore, glorify God in your body" (1 Cor 6:19).

There are a minuscule number of Jews who, supported by American fundamentalists, are actively involved in having the Temple rebuilt and the Cohens and Levys (priests and levites) reinstated to offer animal sacrifice. They think this would inaugurate the Messianic era of peace. More likely it would precipitate the Third World War, since it presumes the obliteration of the Dome of the Rock, the third holiest place in Islam.

The whole area of the Western wall plaza is considered a Holy Place. The inauguration of the Sabbath on Friday evening at sundown is done with a joyful ceremony. Monday and Wednesday mornings are given over to bar mitzvahs amid much cheering and showering of candy on the new "Son of the covenant." Inside the arches are the Arks or Torah cabinets of various synagogues. In the far corner is the entrance to the infamous tunnel dug under the Arab homes and institutions along the wall, ending near the Franciscan Biblical School at the first station.

Vatican Council II and the Jewish People

"The Church of Christ acknowledges that, according to the mystery of God's saving design, the beginnings of her faith and her election are already found among the patriarchs, Moses, and the prophets. She professes that all who believe in Christ, Abraham's children according to faith, are included in the same patriarch's call. . . . The Church, therefore, cannot forget that she received the revelation of the Old Testament through the people with whom God in his inexpressible mercy deigned to establish the Ancient Covenant. Nor can she forget that she draws sustenance from the root of that good olive tree onto which have been grafted the wild olive branches of the Gentiles. Indeed, the Church believes that by His Cross Christ our peace, reconciled Jew and Gentile, making them one in Himself. Also, the Church ever keeps in mind the words of the Apostle about his kinsmen, 'who have the adoption as sons, and the glory and the covenant and the legislation and the worship and the promises; who have the fathers, and from whom is Christ, according to the flesh.'" *Documents of Vatican II,* ed. Walter Abbott, S.J., p. 664.

At this point it would be appropriate to pray, especially while touching the wall, for forgiveness for one's own personal anti-Semitism or that of the Church which has caused so much suffering and tragedy for our brothers and sisters over the centuries. The Good Friday prayer for the perfidious Jews was a sad example of that. Pope John XXIII's revision of it may be prayed:

Prayer

Let us pray for the Jewish people, the first to hear the Word of God, that they may continue to grow in the love of his name and in faithfulness

to his covenant. Almighty and eternal God, long ago you gave your prom-
ise to Abraham and his posterity. Listen to your Church as we pray. May
the people you first chose to be your own be blessed with the fulness of re-
demption. We ask this through Abraham's son and yours, Jesus, our Mes-
siah and Lord. Amen.

The Sacramentary, *Good Friday. General Intercessions, # VI*

Haram esh Sharif (Dome of the Rock)

The Haram, or noble Sanctuary as it is known by the Moslems, was the
site of the threshing floor purchased by David, upon which Solomon built
his temple. Destroyed by the Babylonians in 587, it was rebuilt under the
Persians sixty years later after the return from the exile. With his new retaining walls, Herod expanded the surface to thirty-five acres. His ambitious work on the temple (five thousand priests were trained as stone
masons) was hardly completed when it was destroyed by the Romans in
A.D. 70. Transferring their loyalty from Mount Moriah to Mount Calvary,
the Christians pretty much ignored it.

Mark 13:1-2

> As they were going out of the Temple, one of Jesus' disciples
> brought to his attention the majesty of the building and the splendor
> of the stones. Jesus replied, "Take a good look at this magnificence
> while you can. It won't be long until there's not even one stone on top
> of another."

John 2:18-21

> [After Jesus had cleansed the temple] those in charge demanded a
> sign of authorization for what he had done. His response was: "De-
> stroy this temple and in three days I will raise it up." They countered
> with "It has taken us forty-six years so far to build this temple, and
> you claim that you can raise it in three days?" But he was speaking
> about the temple of his body.

About sixty years after their arrival in Jerusalem (Called by them El
Quds, "the Holy") the Moslems began building the two mosques. The Dome
of the Rock is built over the basalt rock which was thought to be where
Abraham was going to sacrifice his son, Isaac. It was the threshing floor of
Ornan the Jebusite, and later probably served as the base of the altar of
holocausts, southeast of the Temple's entrance.

For the Moslems it commemorates the story of the night ride of Mohammed on his angelic horse from Mecca to Jerusalem from whence he ascended into heaven before his return to Mecca. His regard for Jerusalem was so great that originally he directed that the faithful turn toward El Quds in response to the call to prayer. El Aqsa (means *furthest* which it was from Mecca at the time it was built) has been destroyed by earthquakes many times since it is built not on solid rock, like the Dome, but above the great chambers which Herod built when expanding the plateau of the Temple Mount.

The Crusaders transformed the Dome of the Rock into a church and called it the Temple of Solomon. The Crusader knights worshiped in it while living in El Aqsa and hence they became known as the Knights Templar.

Vatican Council II and the Moslems

"The Church looks with esteem upon the Moslems. They adore the one God, living and enduring, merciful and omnipotent, maker of heaven and earth who speaks his word to us. They strive to submit wholeheartedly even to His inscrutable decrees, just as did Abraham, with whom the Islamic faith is pleased to associate itself. They do not acknowledge Jesus as God, but they revere him as a prophet. They also honor Mary, his virgin mother; and at times they call on her, too, with devotion. In addition they await the day of judgment when God will give each one their due after raising us up. Consequently, they prize the moral life, and give worship to God especially through prayer, almsgiving, and fasting." *Documents of Vatican II,* ed. Walter Abbott, S.J., Declaration on Non-Christians. p. 663.

Prayer

Non-Moslems are not permitted to pray publicly or aloud in the sacred precinct. This is to prevent those Jews who intend to rebuild the temple from establishing a foothold, as has been attempted. However, a moment of silent prayer could be spent begging God's blessing upon this people who strive so mightily to do his will. *SALAAM SHALOM PEACE.*

MODEL OF JERUSALEM

The "City of Peace" has probably suffered more from war than any other in the world. Each time its walls have been rebuilt they have also been moved. Much of the confusion generated by this history of destruction and rebuilding can be dissipated by a visit to the model at the Holy Land Hotel.

The genial architect is in constant consultation with archaeologists and historians to make sure that his work is as accurate and up to date as possible. He builds on a scale of one to fifty, using the same materials that were used in the city as it was thirty years after the sacrifice of Jesus.

HOLOCAUST MEMORIAL (YAD V'SHEM)

The Babylonian exile, from 587–537 B.C., was one of the most devastating events in the history of God's people. Without the temple and the Holy City, many ended in losing their faith in Yahweh. If he existed, he had turned his back on them. To this desperate remnant a prophet (Isa 56:5) promised that contrary to all appearances, the Lord was still with them. As a sign of hope Yahweh pledged to leave in their midst a hand (Yad) and a name (Shem). Both stand for the person. At the time of the Shoah (Holocaust) under Hitler, the surviving Jews recalled this promise. The survivors built this memorial as one of their first acts of faith in their new homeland, the state of Israel.

While the Christian community must constantly apologize for the warped theology and biblical misinterpretation that were used to give legitimacy to the despicable anti-Semitism that made the Holocaust possible, it can also recognize as does the memorial, the role of the "righteous gentiles." Their role in the saving of Jews from certain death is commemorated by the living trees of Yad v'Shem. Among those who worked to save the Jews, Pope Pius XII should not be forgotten. His role was acknowledged by Israel Zolli, the chief Rabbi of Rome who became a Catholic after the war, taking in baptism the name Eugenio, the Pope's own baptismal name.

Part II

Holy Places East of Jerusalem

Holy Places
East of Jerusalem

MOUNT OF OLIVES

The Jerusalemites called it the Mount of Galilee since during the great feasts it became a camp ground for the pilgrims from the North. Jesus and his family would have spent the nights here. Its terrain would have been familiar to him later when he sought a place for prayer in the garden at its base or a place to teach his disciples to pray in the Pater Noster grotto on its summit. It also provided the locale for his weeping over the Holy City, processing to it on Palm Sunday, and his ascending from it a few weeks later.

A quiet place for reflection may still be found in the small park adjacent to the path ascending to the left from the church in the Garden of Gethsemane. Opposite the gate of the garden and church there is a gate into another secluded area opened by the guard on request. For longer periods of reflection and retreats, apply to the Father Guardian of the Convent adjacent to the church. The Franciscans have built hermitages on the other side of the church for just such a purpose.

Mosque of the Ascension

The Moslems have great love and respect for the Prophet Jesus *(Nebi Issa)*. While they do not accept his crucifixion and resurrection, they do believe in his ascension. It is the only Christian holy place that they retain custody of. They permit Christian groups to celebrate liturgy there on the feast of the Ascension. The Gospels do not mention a precise spot for the event, so it can be celebrated here or anywhere on the Mount of Olives.

Luke 24:50-53

> He led them out of the Holy City toward Bethany, lifted up his hands and blessed them. As he did so he was exalted to heaven. They worshiped him and joyfully returned to Jerusalem where they offered their praises to God in the Temple.

Reflection

The message and challenge of the mystery of the Ascension is that while Jesus has returned to the Father, his work must continue. The apostles awaited the gift of the Spirit who empowered them, as the Church, to do just that. With the Ascension begins the third period of Salvation History, the time of the Church. "Just as the Father sent me, so do I send you" (John 20:21).

Pater Noster Church

Jesus may well have taught his disciples to pray at various times and places. The grotto here under the sanctuary of the unfinished church has become a privileged place to recall that Jesus taught us to pray with a new intimacy. It is particularly appropriate since it is the location of a cloistered Carmel, a powerhouse of prayer.

It seems strange that the disciples should have asked Jesus to teach them to pray, since they had a hundred and fifty beautiful prayers called Psalms. But Jesus had brought his disciples into a new and intimate relationship with his Father (the original was Abba which can again be heard on the streets of Jerusalem as a little child calls his "daddy"). The new relationship called for new and intimate language, and no psalm calls God Father, much less Abba.

The beautiful ceramic tiles with the Lord's Prayer in many languages are the work of the Olivetan Benedictine Community of Abu Ghosh. The English is found in the enclosed corridor after the chapel. "Abba Father" may also be sung.

Panorama of Jerusalem

The Old City, Jerusalem

Early pilgrims arriving from the coast caught their first sight of the Holy City from the mountain adjoining the Mount of Olives. In a burst of joy they cried out "Scopeo, scopeo." Thus the Greek for "I see" is said to have given the name to Mount Scopus. The same view and burst of emotion can be had from the observation point above the Brigham Young Jerusalem Campus and in front of the Hebrew University and Hadassah Hospital on Mount Scopus.

Other places for viewing are amidst the camels, donkeys, and peddlers across the road from the Seven Arches Hotel. Below it is a more secluded small amphitheater. The pathway down to and the garden of the chapel of Dominus Flevit might also cause you to cry out "Scopeo" even though you are on the Mount of Olives.

A person who had received a high honor was heard to exclaim, "After this, there's only heaven." The author of the Book of Revelation felt the same way about the Holy City.

Revelation 21:2-4

> There came to me the vision of a new Jerusalem . . . descending from heaven, as radiant as a bride on her wedding day. Then came a voice from the throne which said: "God's dwelling place is with his people, and there he shall be at home, for they are his people, and he is their God. He will dry their tears for death and mourning, weeping and wailing, are gone forever."

Splendid views from the south can be had from the Church of St. Peter in Gallicantu and from the park on the Hill of Evil Counsel, so named not because it is the mid-East headquarters of the United Nations, but because Absalom plotted the revolt against his father David here (2 Samuel 13ff). One of the tombs in the Kidron Valley below is called "Yad Absholom" after David's beloved son who betrayed him.

The graves on the Mount of Olives are Jewish; below the Eastern wall of Jerusalem, on Mount Moriah, they are Moslem; and to the south on Mount Zion, Christian. During the exile (587–537 B.C.) Ezekiel responded to those who felt that they might as well be dead:

Ezekiel 37:12ff

> "Son of Man, these are the bones of my people. 'We are skeletons, we are without hope, we are dead' they are crying. But tell them, I, their God, have an urgent message for them. 'You are my people, and I will cause you to burst forth from your grave and return to the land of Israel. And when I do open your grave, and you come forth from it, then you will really know that I am your God, and you are my people. It is Yahweh who speaks. I will pour forth my spirit upon you and you will come back to life. I swear it, I promise it.'"

Back from Babylon, after the exile, Joel looked upon the Kidron Valley and changed its name to the Valley of Jehoshaphat (Yahweh Judges). "All you nations, run quickly to the Valley of Jehoshaphat for that is where you will hear Yahweh's judgment on you proclaimed" (4:12).

After Jesus declared that religious hypocrites were like graves that were beautiful externally, but inside stunk of death (Matt 23:27ff), he proclaimed what evidence God would use in arriving at a verdict in the judgment. And it was not scrupulous observance of the laws of religion.

Matthew 25:31-46

> When the Son of Man is manifested in all of his glory, and surrounded by legions of angels he will preside over the gathering of the peoples. He will divide them, just as you have seen a shepherd put the sheep on his right and the goats on his left. Then the King will decide who goes where. To those on his right, he will say: "My Father is delighted with you. Come and claim the inheritance that he has willed for you." Why? What did you do to deserve it? Because . . . .

Hymn: *Whatsoever You Do* (page 170)

Palm Sunday

Although the Gospels state that Jesus began his trip at Bethany and Bethphage on the Mount of Olives, most pilgrims will be satisfied to re-enact that part which is the descent beginning at the Latin shrine of *Dominus Flevit* ("the Lord wept"), to the Garden of Gethsemane with the view across the valley to the Golden Gate which Jesus entered.

Dominus Flevit

This shrine, commemorating the tears Jesus shed because of the smug complacency of the "religious" people, is one of the calmest and most peaceful of all of the Holy Places. The extensive and well-kept grounds are conducive to prayer and even to tears if you are so inclined.

To the right, inside the entrance, the archaeologists from the Franciscan Biblical School at the first station on the Via Dolorosa have excavated an ancient burial cave. Space was at a premium, so occupancy of a grave was only for a year. At that time the skeleton was placed on top of the bones of one's ancestors in a hollow in the center of the grotto. This gave rise to the circumlocution of death as being "gathered" to one's ancestors. A later generation, with more emphasis on the individual and less on the community, placed the bones in ossuaries which are so much in evidence. The temporary occupancy of the burial niche helps make sense of the statement in the Gospels that Jesus' body was placed in a tomb in which they did not have to remove a skeleton to make room for him. It was new and that was unusual; but then, on the third day he did not need it anymore.

The chapel is built on the site of a Byzantine one that faced east. In those days every church faced the rising sun as a visible remembrance of the risen Son. The architect Barluzzi reversed the direction so as to have the panorama of Jerusalem with the grey dome of the Holy Sepulcher visible to the right of the golden dome.

Luke 19:28-45

> Jesus continued on his pilgrimage up to Jerusalem until he came near the villages of Bethany and Bethphage on the Mount of Olives. He sent two of his disciples into the village where they were to find the colt of a donkey and bring it to him, even though it had not been broken in. If any one questioned them they were simply to say: "The Master has need of it." And that's exactly what happened. They threw their own cloaks on the beast and Jesus mounted it. As he was about to descend the mountain, the whole group of his disciples became a

joyful chorus, praising God for his amazing deeds. "The King comes in the name of the Lord. Blessed be he. God's glory descends from heaven. His peace falls like the rain."

Some of the Pharisees had mingled in and asked him to exercise his authority as a teacher and impose silence on his disciples. His reply? "If my disciples grow silent, the very stones will take up the chorus!" When Jerusalem came into sight, he broke into tears and lamented, "If only this day you would finally recognize what will bring you peace. But you just cannot see. But I can see that the time is coming when your enemies will build ramparts around your walls and choke you. Both you and your children will be smashed to the ground and when they are finished with you, one stone will not be left on another. And when you ask why, remember that it was because you just did not recognize the time of your visitation." Then he entered into the temple area.

Reflection

As we try to put ourselves into this dramatic picture, each figure has a message or a challenge for us. One that is not so obvious has been caught by Gilbert Keith Chesterton in this poem.

The Donkey

When fishes flew and forests walked, and figs grew upon thorn,
Some moment when the moon was blood, then surely I was born;
With monstrous head and sickening cry, and ears like errant wings,
The devil's walking parody of all four-footed things.
The tattered outlaw of the earth, of ancient crooked will;
Starve, scourge, deride me: I am dumb, I keep my secret still.
Fools! For I also had my hour; one far fierce hour and sweet:
There was a shout about my ears, and palms before my feet.

Hymns: During the walk down the Mount of Olives, re-enacting Palm Sunday, familiar hymns that people will recall from memory may be sung. It is not easy to try to read from a book and watch your step (or wallet or purse!) at the same time. A cantor or two may help with everyone joining in the refrain. Suggestions: *Holy, Holy, Holy! Lord God Almighty* (page 163); *Amazing Grace* (page 156); *The Holy City* (page 161); *How Great Thou Art* (page 163); *The King of Glory* (page 164); *Battle Hymn of the Republic* (page 157); *Holy God, We Praise Thy Name* (page 162)

The route down from the Mount of Olives passes by the Russian Orthodox Convent of St. Mary Magdalene. The onion-shaped domes of its church, soaring heavenward, remind us of the rich spirituality of the Church of the East, so much of which recently emerged from its passion under communism.

Garden of Gethsemane

Olive grove on Mount of Olives, Jerusalem

Hopefully pilgrims have seized places to meditate on the last hours of Jesus, for it is next to impossible to do it here where he did. For many reasons, The Church of All Nations in the Garden of Gethsemane is the most popular of the Holy Places, with non-stop liturgies and wall-to-wall crowds of tourists (some of whom are pilgrims). However, directly opposite the entrance is a gate to a secluded spot which the guard will usually open upon request. Also, the grotto which tradition holds that Jesus used for prayer is down the passageway, to the right of the tomb of Mary, and this is a blessed find for peace and quiet.

The Garden of Gethsemane (*Gat Shemen* is Hebrew for olive press) contains trees the roots of which go back to the time when Jesus prayed here. It is almost impossible to kill an olive tree. If cut down, a new one shoots forth from the roots. Its branches are the symbol of peace, shalom. The word has a very rich meaning. It is the Hebrew word used in the text of Isaiah 53:5: "He bore the suffering that makes us *whole*." Shalom means to be complete or entire. It has the connotation of being everything that a person should be and living up to all the promise that is within each of us.

> [Jesus Christ] is our shalom. He has brought us together . . . thus making shalom. His greeting to all, both far and near, is shalom (Eph 2:14ff passim). On the evening of the first day of the week, Jesus came to where the disciples were huddled in fear and greeted them: "Shalom, again, I say to you. Shalom" (John 20:19).

But it is good to remember in this place where the olive branches speak of peace, Jesus' suffering and death must come first.

The somber interior of the church, with its purple-tinted windows, provides the atmosphere of the story that is told in the mosaics. They tell us of disciples who are indifferent, of the Son of God who is tempted while at prayer, of the angel who comforts, of the traitor who uses the sign of love to betray, and of the religious leaders who are threatened, and so bring their soldiers.

Luke 22:39-53

> Jesus left the room where he had celebrated the Passover, and went with his disciples to the Mount of Olives. Before going off by himself, he told them to pray that they might not be tempted beyond their ability to resist. Falling on his knees, he begged: "Father, I don't want to go through with this, but your will, not mine be done." He was totally absorbed in prayer, and his perspiration poured off him like drops of blood. An angel came to give him some encouragement. Then he got up and returned to the disciples, only to find that grief had thrown them into a deep sleep. "What's going on," he asked them? "Shake yourselves and just hope and pray that you'll be able to handle what's coming."
>
> He scarcely had the words out of his mouth when Judas, one of his twelve apostles appeared at the head of a mob. He started to embrace Jesus, who said to him, "Judas, are you going to betray me by kissing me?" . . . To those who had come for him, Jesus said, "Am I a common criminal that you come after me armed to the teeth? When I was right in your midst, teaching day after day in the temple, you never lifted a finger against me. But, this is your hour. It is the hour of darkness."

Reflection

When one is attacked by an enemy, at least one knows why. It is not difficult to comprehend the enmity of the religious leaders. It was a question of job security. If Jesus was the way, the truth and the life, then they were out of a job. They perceived him as a great danger to established religion, and they were the establishment.

But when you had only twelve friends to stick by you, and eleven fell asleep after you begged for their support, and the twelfth feigned loyalty while plotting against you, then you know what it is to be abandoned and forsaken. This, too, is the cross. This is what Jesus embraced when he embraced our humanity. This is the world the Father so loved that he sent his only begotten Son.

Prayer of Abandonment

Father, I abandon myself into your hands! Do with me what you will; whatever you may do, I thank you. I am ready for all, I accept all. Let only your will be done in me and in all your creatures. I wish no more than this, O Lord. Into your hands I commend my spirit: I offer it to you with all the love of my heart, for I love you, Lord, and so need to give myself, to surrender myself into your hands, without reserve, and with boundless confidence, for you are my Father.

Charles de Foucald
(On a prayer card from the Poor Clares in Nazareth where he was the gardener)

Hymns: *Amazing Grace* (page 156); *Were You There When They Crucified My Lord?* (page 169)

BETHANY

On the Jericho Road at the edge of the Judean Desert is the village of Jericho which the Arabs call El Azarya after one of its most famous citizens, Lazarus. The church, amid the Crusader and Byzantine ruins is on the main road, below the Orthodox Church and the mosque built over the "tomb of Lazarus."

The Gospels mention three incidents in the life of Jesus as having occurred here, at the home of his friends, Martha, Mary, and Lazarus. If liturgy is not being celebrated, the events may be illustrated by the splendid mosaics on the walls of the church. (If reading aloud, do so slowly and deliberately, since the acoustics are not the best.)

[**Behind the Altar**] *"Lazarus of Bethany, the brother of Martha and Mary was very sick. . . . When Jesus arrived, he found that Lazarus had already been four days in the grave. . . . Martha rushed out to meet him and told him that if he had been there her brother would still be alive. Jesus told her that her brother would rise again, and she said that she already knew that he would rise on the last day. Jesus said: 'I am the* *resurrection and the life; whoever believes in me, even if they die, they will live forever.'. . . Martha said: 'You are the messiah. You are the Son of God'* " (John 11:17ff).

[**Right**] *"Jesus prayed, 'Father, you have never failed me. Thank you.' Then he cried out: 'Lazarus, come forth!' But he was still bound up in the burial cloths, so Jesus said to the mourners, 'Unbind him and let him go free'"* (John 11:38ff).

[**Rear**] *"While Jesus was in Bethany at the house of Simon the Leper, reclining at the dinner table, a woman approached him. From an alabaster jar she poured forth aromatic oil upon his head. Judas protested about the flagrant waste, but Jesus insisted that it was no waste when it was preparing his body for burial . . . and added that what she had done would be proclaimed as part of the gospel throughout the whole world in memory of her"* (Matt 26:6-13 passim).

[**Left**] *"Mary took a position at the feet of the Lord, listening to him. Martha stuck her head out of the kitchen and said: 'Lord, doesn't it bother you, too, that my sister isn't lifting a finger to help me? Tell her to get busy.' But the Lord answered, 'Martha, Martha, you are so preoccupied with those things. But Mary chose this. It is far more important, and I will not deprive her of it'"* (Luke 10:38-42 passim).

Reflection

The movie *Yentl* illustrated well how the study of the Torah, under the aegis of a rabbi, was a male prerogative. Never would a self-respecting rabbi allow a woman to take the position of a disciple at his feet. This story is a vivid illustration of Paul's emancipation proclamation: "We are all one in Christ Jesus so that there is no longer such a thing as Jew or Gentile, slave or free, male or female" (Gal 3:28). If only we were aware how radical Jesus was.

Prayer

In this home of Martha, Mary, and Lazarus, whose friendship and hospitality Jesus so enjoyed, we, whom Jesus also called his friends, make known our needs to his Father.

Response: **Lord, hear our prayer** *(sung)*

For all of our friends, that God may bless them for sharing their lives with us . . .

For the peoples of this land who have shown us such gracious hospitality . . .

For women everywhere, that they may be empowered to use fully the gifts that God has given them . . .

For all the women who have brought us closer to Christ . . .

For all whom the Lord has called to the single state, that his kingdom may come because of their singleness of heart . . .

That we, like Lazarus may through our deaths be restored to life with Jesus . . .

God, after whom every family in heaven and on earth is named, bless us who are now guests in this home. Here, your son Jesus found the companionship and joy of a loving family. May all who visit our homes find him there also. We ask this through Christ the Lord.

QUMRAN

Qumran was a settlement of the Jewish sect of the Essenes in the inhospitable wilderness bordering the Dead Sea, where the famous scrolls were discovered in 1947. The eleven caves in the adjacent hillside yielded their treasure, including fragments of every book of the Hebrew Bible except Esther, and many non-biblical documents as well. They date from before the destruction of Jerusalem by Titus. Most are not scrolls, but fragments mixed with bat dung and the dust of millennia. Scholars are still at work on them, trying to learn more about the world into which Christianity was born and what may be the possible relationship, if any, between the two groups.

MASADA

Thirty miles south, Masada is the site of the famous fortification that Herod the Great built on a mesa adjacent to the Dead Sea. The Zealots took it by stealth from the Roman garrison, and held it against the might of the Empire for three years after the fall of Jerusalem. While not a religious site for a Christian pilgrimage, the story is fascinating and paramount to the history of the Jewish people. "Masada never again" is the triumphant cry of their survival and freedom.

JERICHO

After the barrenness of the Desert of Judea, and the funereal waters of the Dead Sea, the lowest spot on the face of the earth, one appreciates more than ever what an oasis is. The riotous color of the flowers and the abundance of fresh fruit and vegetables heighten the impression of a place of refreshment. It is also a symbol of pride and new life for the Palestinian people, since it is the first part of their land returned to them. Here, on the site of the oldest continuously inhabited city on the earth, a new nation is coming to birth (not without labor pains!).

Zacchaeus and the Sycamore

Among the biblical relics that are pointed out is an ancient sycamore tree, a descendent, obviously of the one that provided a perch and listening post for the diminutive tax collector upon whom Luke conferred immortality in his Gospel.

Luke 19:1-10

> **Narrator:** Jesus was on his way up to Jerusalem, and he was passing through Jericho. One of the inhabitants of the city was named Zacchaeus. He collected taxes for the Romans and had done rather well at it. He was shorter than most, so in order to catch a glimpse of Jesus, he ran ahead of the crowd, and scampered up a sycamore tree overlooking where Jesus would pass. When Jesus got to the spot, he stood still and looked up.
>
> **Jesus:** "Zacchaeus! Come on down. You have a guest for the night—me!"
>
> **Narrator:** Zacchaeus leaped down and gave Jesus a big welcome. A buzz arose from those who had been checking out the scene. Among the whispers was heard: "Look what kind of person he's staying with." That didn't bother Zacchaeus.
>
> **Zacchaeus:** "Lord, half of all my possessions are going to the poor. And if there has been any cheating on my part, I'll give fourfold to anyone I have taken advantage of."
>
> **Jesus:** "This very day salvation has come to this house. Do you want to see a genuine son of Abraham? Take a look at him. This is the very reason why the Son of Man came. My mission is to search for and to find what was lost."

In and Around Jericho

Tel es Sultan. The archaeological mound of Jericho is composed of the many levels of war and destruction at the site. 'Josue fit the battle of Jericho and the walls came tumblin down' may be based more on folklore (God can inspire that, too, pace the fundamentalists) than on history, since no evidence of the fall of the walls during the priests' parade has been found as yet.

Mount of Temptation. Clinging to the mountain west of Jericho is the monastery that commemorates the temptation of Jesus "up a high mountain where he could see all the kingdoms of the world and the glory thereof" in Matthew and Luke. The level top of the mountain is the foundation of a projected Orthodox church.

Church of the Good Shepherd. The Catholics of Jericho are served by the church and school (Our Lady of Jericho) staffed by the Franciscan Friars and Sisters.

Mount Nebo. On the eastern shore of the Dead Sea is the spot where Moses died before he could enter into the Promised Land. Recent excavations by the archaeologists of the Franciscan Biblical School of the Flagellation in Jerusalem have uncovered splendid mosaics of the Byzantine Period.

Place of Baptism. The Gospels are not clear as to where the baptism of Jesus took place, and the spot that is celebrated near Jericho is usually not accessible due to military considerations. A kibbutz has built a fine place near where the waters of the Sea of Galilee flow into the River Jordan.

Part III

Holy Places West of Jerusalem

Holy Places
West of Jerusalem

EIN KAREM

Once a village of hundreds of Christian families, this charming little town is a good example of what will happen if the emigration of the Christian Palestinians continues throughout the land. The families fled from here during the 1948 War. They were not permitted to return and their homes were lost. Now the only Christians are the custodians of the Holy Places and the staffs of the church's charitable works, such as the boys' orphanage on the road to the shrine of the Visitation. If you can't stop to say hello to the Sisters of the Rosary, a native Palestinian community, at least leave an alms for their holy innocents or buy a gift from the sister at the stand on the way back.

Church of the Visitation

The "spring in the vineyard" (Ein Karem) after which the town was named was recently renovated by the Rothschilds. Up the path, past the Rosary Sisters' orphanage and the Russian Orthodox Convent, is the Church of the Visitation, with its small Byzantine grotto-chapel and well on the first level. On the right is the rock that swallowed the Baptist so that he would not become one of the Holy Innocents. The story is found in the apocryphal proto-evangelium of James, and is illustrated in the fresco above. (And as has been wisely stated: If it isn't true, it's still a good story.) Around the courtyard the Magnificat is found in many languages. If there are enough who remember the mother tongue, the Latin lyrics are also found above the frescoed scenes in the upper church. (Courage, just a few more steps!)

There, in the apse, behind the altar is depicted Mary coming over the hill country of Judea to be greeted by the then patriarch of Jerusalem, Alberto Gori, O.F.M. (Franciscan bishops used to wear grey). The custos of the Holy Land presents a model of the church for her approval. In the left panel the faithful present the Marian shrines of Europe, and on the right are members of those religious communities dedicated to our Lady under different titles (Carmel, Visitation, etc.).

The side panels depict (1) the Council of Ephesus where she was proclaimed the Mother of God; (2) mother of the whole Church whose representatives are shown under her mantle, including the architect Barluzzi, staring out and wearing a bow tie; (3) the Wedding Feast of Cana where she interceded for the couple as she does for us today; (4) the Battle of Lepanto where the Moslems were kept from conquering Europe and she was given the title "Our Lady, Help of Christians;" and (5) the disputation of Blessed John duns Scotus and the Franciscan theologians with the Dominicans who denied the Immaculate Conception. On the way out notice the figures of the two pregnant women on the bronze doors.

Prayer

The second Joyful Mystery of the Rosary, The Visitation of Mary who came from Nazareth to be with her elderly cousin Elizabeth in the last trimester of her pregnancy. (The text of the Magnificat in Latin is painted above the frescoes and windows.)

Hymns: *Hail Mary, Gentle Woman* (page 160); *Magnificat* (page 166)

Church of the Nativity of John the Baptist

Grotto of birth of John the Baptist, Ein Karem

The church has had a tradition of being under the patronage of the Royal Family of Spain as evidenced by the azuelos (tiles) covering the walls, numerous masterpieces attributed to great Spanish artists or their schools, and the coat of arms over the door. Through the sacristy there is an exposition of the art, vestments, and memorabilia showered upon the church over the years. To the left of the sanctuary the stairs descend to the traditional place where the inscription under the altar says *Hic Praecursor Domini Natus Est* ("Here the forerunner of the Lord was born").

Luke 1:68-78. ICEL: Prayer of the Hours

> Elizabeth, when her time came, gave birth to a son. His father Zachary wrote "He shall be called John". . . . All who heard were amazed and wondered what the future would hold for this child, for surely the hand of the Lord was with him. Then his father, filled with the Holy Spirit, prophesied:
>
> Blessed be the Lord, the God of Israel; he has come to his people and set them free.
>
> He has raised up for us a mighty savior, born of the house of his servant David.
>
> Through his holy prophets he promised of old that he would save us from our enemies, from the hands of all who hate us.
>
> He promised to show mercy to our fathers and to remember his holy covenant.
>
> This was the oath he swore to our father Abraham: to set us free from the hands of our enemies,
>
> free to worship him without fear, holy and righteous in his sight all the days of our life.
>
> You, my child, shall be called the prophet of the Most High; for you will go before the Lord to prepare his way, to give his people knowledge of salvation by the forgiveness of our sins.
>
> In the tender compassion of our God the dawn from on high shall break upon us, to shine on those who dwell in darkness and the shadow of death, and to guide our feet into the way of peace.

Hymn: *O Come, O Come, Emmanuel* (page 174)

Chagal Windows

The synagogue of the Hadassah Hospital contains one of the great masterpieces in the history of art, the windows of the twelve tribes of Israel by Marc Chagal (cf. Jacob's testament to his twelve sons, Genesis 49). A visit is ordinarily done by appointment and with a guide provided by the Hospital.

EMMAUS

The only ones who knew exactly where they were going when they set out for Emmaus for the past two thousand years seem to have been Cleopas and his companion (wife?). Today there are three candidates: (1) Latroun is a lovely spot where the Word has been burning in the hearts of Trappists for over one hundred years; (2) at Abu Gosh one may enjoy a wonderful experience in recognizing him in the breaking of the bread. The Olivetan Benedictine community of monks and nuns celebrates with a prayerfulness and a beauty that are beyond description; (3) at Imwas Qubeibe one can walk on the Roman road excavated by the Franciscans. Most were Italians, and so they were held here under house arrest during World War II. They excavated the entire property, especially the remains of the village alongside the road that ran from Jerusalem to the coast. One is not faced with a dilemma since if you have the time, all three are worth a visit. At the Franciscans, one can even break bread by way of a picnic with the facilities provided, with gazelles and peacocks for companions. Be sure to take with you a loaf of bread to break and share during the telling of the story.

Luke 24:13-35

Narrator: On the very same day [that the women found the tomb empty] two of them were headed back home to Emmaus, a village only a few miles from Jerusalem. They were deep in conversation about what had gone on. Without warning, Jesus caught up to them, but they failed to recognize him.

Jesus: "What are you so deeply preoccupied with as you're walking along?"

Disciples: "You have got to be the only one around here who hasn't a clue as to what has been going on."

Jesus: "Well, tell me about it."

Disciples: "What happened to Jesus from Nazareth who was a great prophet sent by God. He had attracted quite a following but the authorities thought they knew better so they got him condemned and crucified. That dashed our hopes that he was the redeemer of Israel. But incredibly, just this morning, some women from our group went to the tomb but his body was not there. And this is the third day since it all happened. And (can you believe it?) they even came back to us and reported seeing angels who claimed he was alive. A few of us went to check it out, and were amazed to find out that the women were right. It was just as they said; he was not there."

Jesus: "How obtuse can you be! Why is it that you are so reluctant to take the prophets' messages seriously? Didn't you know that such suffering must come first if the Messiah is going to enter into his glory?"

Narrator: Then he went through the words of Moses and every prophet and showed them how he was the real meaning of the whole of the Scriptures. As they got close to the village he gave the impression that it was not his destination.

Disciples: "Please, please, come in and stay with us. It is getting dark and it's too late to be on the road."

Narrator: And so he went in and stayed with them. While they were having dinner, he took bread, blessed it, broke it and gave it to them. With that they knew who he was, but he disappeared, and they saw him no longer.

Disciples: "How he set our hearts on fire as he spoke to us and opened up the meaning of God's word."

Narrator: They wasted no time in returning to Jerusalem, but before they could get a word out of their mouths they heard the news from the eleven and the others with them:

All: He is risen, he is risen, he is risen.

Narrator: After they had declared that Simon had actually seen him, the two disciples told of their own experience and how they, too, had recognized him in the breaking of the bread.

All: Alleluia Alleluia Alleluia.

The Lord Jesus is present to us in the community, in the Word, and in the breaking of the bread. This profound mystery presented by Luke in such a wonderful story needs no further elaboration but does cry out for quiet contemplation. After a few minutes a eucharistic hymn may be sung, e.g., *I Am the Bread of Life* (page 164).

Part IV

Holy Places South of Jerusalem

Holy Places
South of Jerusalem

ON THE ROAD TO BETHLEHEM

To get from Jerusalem to Bethlehem you have to pass through hell. The Hinnon Valley, west of Jerusalem was where the unfaithful messiahs, like Achaz (2 Kings 16:3) sacrificed their sons to the idols. Despised by the prophets, the place became the smoky, smelly, foul analogy for hell. The Valley of Hinnon (Hebrew: Gai Hinnon) became Gehenna. As you pass through, notice the place for concerts, the movie theater, and restaurants. Hell doesn't look all that bad, but I wouldn't take a chance!

A left turn after the wall of the Poor Clares leads to the Hill of Evil Counsel with its view of Jerusalem from the south. Continuing on the main road, the Orthodox Monastery of St. Elias on the left commemorates the story of 1 Kings 19 where Elijah was fed by the angel to give him strength for his forty-day journey to meet Yahweh at Sinai (Horeb). Nearby, recent road work uncovered the mosaic of the ancient Church of the Kathisma where legend has it that Mary rested on the Bethlehem road. Willingly or not, the pilgrim must do the same today in order to pass through the Israeli check point. Unless you are visiting early in the morning, it is impossible to find peace and quiet here.

Tomb of Rachel

The 15-minute ride to Bethlehem passes by Tantur, the ecumenical-theological center established by Pope Paul VI and run by Notre Dame University. At the approach to the "Little Town" is the Tomb of Rachel.

Matthew 2:16-18

> Once Herod realized that he had been deceived by the astrologers,
> he became furious. He ordered the massacre of all the boys two years

old and under in Bethlehem and its environs, making his calculations on the basis of the date he had learned from the astrologers. What was said through Jeremiah the prophet was then fulfilled:

> "A cry was heard at Ramah,
> sobbing and loud lamentation:
> Rachel bewailing her children;
> no comfort for her,
> since they are no more."

Church of the Nativity

Manger Square, with its merchants of carved olive wood creches and mother-of-pearl jewelry, stands in front of one of the most ancient churches of Christendom. It is in the charge of the Greek Orthodox. Centuries ago the spacious door was reduced to the small one of today so that one must bow low to enter the spot where God humbled himself to become man. It was done for a less spiritual reason: to prevent looting invaders from riding in on horseback. The interior of the church still contains elements from the fourth-century Church of St. Helena, such as the mosaic floor beneath the wooden doors of the present level. To the right of the Orthodox sanctuary a staircase descends to the cave of the Nativity. The silver star beneath the Greek altar proclaims in Latin that "Here the Word was made Flesh." To the side are the Latin altars of the Manger and the Adoration by the Magi.

Shrine of the Nativity, Bethlehem

Luke 2:1-7

> In those days Caesar Augustus published a decree ordering a census of the whole world. This first census took place while Quirinius was governor of Syria. Everyone went to register, each to his own town. And so Joseph went from the town of Nazareth in Galilee to Judea, to David's town of Bethlehem . . . because he was of the house and lineage of David . . . to register with Mary, his espoused wife, who was with child.
>
> While they were there the days of her confinement were completed. She gave birth to her first-born son and wrapped him in swaddling clothes and laid him in a manger, because there was no room for them in the place where travelers lodged.

Reflection

Kneel before the place where the "Word was made flesh and dwelt among us." Know that he loved us so much that "he became like us in everything!" There is no part of our humanity that he did not embrace. He loved and laughed and cried and cringed. He sweated and sighed. Surely Augustine is right when he said that the only line of the New Testament that is so unique that it can be found nowhere else is "The Word was made flesh and dwelt among us." He shared our humanity that we might share his divinity.

Prayer

Father, we kneel before him who is the image of the invisible God, the firstborn of all creation (Col 1). Here, your eternal plan is fulfilled. We fall on our knees before him for whom you made the universe. He is the world's center of gravity and the very heartbeat of creation. Thank you for the overflowing love which burst forth and is found in the arms of Mary. With the fire of that love, melt the iciness of our hearts that we may proclaim "Jesus is Lord." Amen.

Hymns: *Silent Night, Holy Night* (page 175); *O Come, All Ye Faithful* (page 174)

Church of St. Catherine

Ascending the stairs to the left brings us to the area where the Armenian Orthodox worship, and to the entrance to the Church of St. Catherine. Since history has deprived the Latin Rite Catholics of all but a tiny area of the basilica, beside it they have built their parish church dedicated to the Patroness of Philosophers, St. Catherine of Alexandria. Often there is a quiet corner in this church from whence Christmas midnight Mass is televised, or in front of the courtyard of St. Jerome where one can contemplate the mystery of God's love in the birth of his Son. The following may be helpful.

Reflection

The Solemn Proclamation of the Nativity is chanted in monasteries on Christmas Eve.

From the beginning of time, when Yahweh, our God spoke his creative word over the chaos, saying: "Let there be light"—5,199 years.

From the spread of sin upon the earth when Yahweh, our God cleaned his creation in the waters of the flood—2,957 years.

From the birth of Abraham, our father in faith—1,850 years.

From the Passover of the children of Israel when they passed over from the wintertime of slavery to the springtime of God's love—1,250 years.

From the anointing of David, God's chosen messiah—1,000 years.

In the sixty-fifth week according to the prophecy of Daniel, according to the calendar of the Greek Empire—the 194th olympiad.

According to the calendar of the Roman empire, from the founding of the city of Rome—752 years.

From the commencement of the reign of the Emperor Augustus—42 years.

In the sixth epoch of the universe, while the whole world rejoiced in peace, Jesus Christ, Eternal God and Son of the Eternal Father, desiring to restore all things to himself and to rekindle love in the universe that was made for him was conceived by the power of the Holy Spirit. Then, after nine months in the womb of Holy Mary, his virgin mother, THE WORD WAS MADE FLESH AND DWELT AMONG US.

Let us celebrate the birth of our Lord Jesus Christ according to the flesh!

Trans: Stephen C. Doyle, O.F.M.
from the Roman Martyrology

In the rear of the Church of St. Catherine are the steps to the other grottos connected to that of the Church of the Nativity. At the foot of the stairway is the Grotto of St. Joseph, to the left is that of the Holy Innocents. To the right is the cave where St. Jerome's remains were interred before being taken to Rome by the Crusaders. The cave beyond, said to be where he translated the Hebrew and Greek of the Bible into the Latin Vulgate, has a mosaic of himself and his friends. The book has the most famous words of his translation, the first line of the prologue of St. John (1:1-5; 10-13):

IN PRINCIPIO ERAT VERBUM.

"In the beginning was the Word and the Word was with God and the Word was God. In the beginning he was with God. Through him all things came into existence. Without him there was nothing. In him was life, and that life was the light of all; the light shines through the darkness, and the darkness was helpless against it.

He was in the world, the very world that came into existence through him, but that world did not recognize him. He came to his own, but his own were not open to him. But to all who were open to him, he gave the power to become God's own children. They were the ones who did believe in his name. And they became God's own children not because of any human act or decision. It came about by the power of God himself.

AND THE WORD WAS MADE FLESH AND DWELT AMONG US.

We were witnesses of his glory, the glory that belongs to him as the only begotten Son of the Father, and in his grace we have all participated, grace after grace after grace. There is no denying that the Law came through Moses, but it remained for Jesus Christ to be the fount of grace and of truth. Human eyes have never caught even a glimpse of God. But God the only begotten Son who abides in the heart of the Father has revealed him to us."

Reflection

". . . God's Word, by whom all things were made, was Himself made flesh so that as perfect man He might save all . . . and sum up all things in Himself. The Lord is the goal of human history, the focal point of the longings of history and of civilization, the center of the human race, the joy of every heart, and the answer to all its yearnings. He it is whom the Father raised from the dead, lifted on high, and stationed at His right hand, making Him Judge of the living and the dead. Enlivened and united in His Spirit, we journey toward the consummation of human history, which fully accords with the counsel of God's love: 'To re-establish all things in Christ, both those in the heavens and those on the earth' (Eph 1:10).

"The Lord Himself speaks: 'Behold, I come quickly! And my reward is with me, to render to each one according to his works. I am the Alpha and the Omega, the first and the last, the beginning and the end' (Apoc. 22:12-13)."

Vatican II: Church Today: Abbott p. 247

Shepherd's Field

To find the peace so necessary for prayer, go to Shepherd's Field out-side the city. Here, where shepherds traditionally tended their sheep, is a cave where liturgy may be celebrated after arrangement. There is a lovely chapel donated by Canadian Catholics. The friar in attendance will usually give permission to ring the bells while you sing the Gloria.

Luke 2:8-18

> There were shepherds in that locality, living in the fields and keep-ing night watch by turns over their flocks. The angel of the Lord ap-peared to them as the glory of the Lord shone around them, and they were very much afraid. The angel said to them: "You have nothing to fear! I come to proclaim good news to you—tidings of great joy to be shared by the whole people. This day in David's city a savior has been born to you, the Messiah and Lord. Let this be a sign to you: in a manger you will find an infant wrapped in swaddling clothes."

Reflection

"The Glory of God is man fully alive" (St. Irenaeus). To be fully alive! This was no longer a dream, for the Son of God had come "That they may have life and have it abundantly" (John 10:10). The news did not come to the priests. It did not come to King Herod. It came to the shepherds, poor-est of the poor, migrant workers and outcasts of society.

They were looked down upon, but in their night vigils they had been looking up at the sky, the moon, and the stars. They had watched the mir-acle of lambs being born. They never lost their sense of wonder at crea-tion, so they were close to their Creator. Suddenly they were invited to the New Creation in Christ the Lord. They were told that the age of Peace had dawned. In Aramaic, the language of Jesus, peace is "Shalom." It means to be complete, to be whole, to be everything you are capable of becoming, to be fully alive to the glory of God.

Prayer

Almighty God and Father of our Lord Jesus Christ, the light has come into the darkness and the darkness could not overpower it. It is the fullness of time. It is the apex of history and only a few shepherds were open enough to be told of it. We join our faith with theirs, and our voices with the angels: "Glory to God in the highest." Grant to us that peace which the angels announced. We ask this in the name of Jesus, the Lord. Amen.

Hymn: *Angels We Have Heard on High* (page 172)

HEBRON

The combination mosque-synagogue testifies to the fact that Abraham, whom Christians revere as our father in faith, is jointly honored by Arab and Jew as their common ancestor. The building, from Herod's time, is built over the cave of Machpelah which Abraham bought to serve as a tomb. There, the patriarchs and some of their wives were interred.

Genesis 25:7-11

The whole span of Abraham's life was one hundred and seventy-five years. Then he breathed his last, dying at a ripe old age, grown old after a full life; and he was gathered to his ancestors. His sons Isaac and Ishmael buried him in the cave of Machpelah in the field of Ephron, son of Zohar the Hittite, which faces Mamre, the field that Abraham bought from the Hittites; there he was buried next to his wife Sarah. After the death of Abraham, God blessed his son Isaac.

Part V

Holy Places North of Jerusalem

Holy Places
North of Jerusalem

SAMARIA

In the Holy Land, there are three routes that run north and south. The Via Maris was the most important commercial route since it ran from Egypt, through the Sinai and Palestine along the Mediterranean Sea, and then turned east through the plain of Megiddo to the Sea of Galilee and then on up to the empires of the Fertile Crescent along the Tigris and Euphrates rivers. The eastern route went right down the Jordan rift valley and was fortified even in the time of Saul by a fortress at Beth Shean. Herod fortified the southern part against Egyptian attack by his fortresses on either side of the Dead Sea at Machaerus and Massada.

The route through Samaria in the center of the country was avoided then because of enmity with the local populace, and today because of the Jewish settlements in the occupied territories that are the occasions of so much tension (cf. Appendix 2: Samaritans). Apparently the early Christian community did not inherit the antagonism toward the Samaritans that was endemic to popular Judaism. Luke 9:52ff. does relate an unpleasant incident when one Samaritan village refused hospitality out of principle since Jesus and his followers were heading for Jerusalem. But every other mention of the Samaritans in the Gospels is positive: the woman at the well (John 4), the good Samaritan (Luke 10), the grateful leper who was a Samaritan (Luke 17:11). Acts 8 tells us that the very first missionary effort of the infant Church was to the Samaritan community and was highly successful (in spite of Matt 10:5). According to some scholars, it may have been the locale where the core writing that later developed into the Gospel of St. John was written. Even if you are not passing through Samaria, the wonderful story of John 4 should be the object of prayer for any pilgrim.

MEGIDDO

The lush and fertile plain that separates Samaria from Galilee is called Megiddo, also known as the valley of Jezreel. Strategically situated between Egypt and the empires of the north (Hittite, Syrian, Babylonian, Assyrian, neo-Babylonian, and Persian, before the Greeks and Romans moved in!), it unfortunately became more famous for its battles than for its agriculture. The northern kingdom of Israel was frequently drawn into them, becoming more preoccupied with the military industrial complex than with its God. To show disgust at the constant fighting, Yahweh told the prophet Hosea to name his son after the valley: "Give him the name Jezreel, for in a little while I will punish the royal dynasty of the northern kingdom for the carnage at Jezreel" (1:4). The poor kid. That's like going through life with the name "Pearl Harbor."

The reputation of the valley for battles and bloodshed was so tenacious that the author of Revelation took "Hill of Megiddo" (Hebrew: *Har Magiddo*) and made it into Armageddon (Rev 16:16). Here is the battlefield for the last great conflict of history. Hopefully the next to the last one was during World War I when General Allenby of Great Britain defeated the Ottoman Empire here in 1918 and was honored with the title "Lord Allenby of Megiddo." Today the archaeological excavations of fortifications from the time of Solomon continue. Levels of habitation previous to him and following him have been uncovered providing the material for James Michener's epic historical novel, *The Source*.

MOUNT CARMEL

The long and majestic range of Carmel (Kerem El = Vineyard of God) stretches from the mountains of Samaria all the way to the Mediterranean. The Carmelite Friary at Muhraqa on the eastern end has spectacular views. The names, directions, and distances to various sites are marked on the terrace. Whether on the terrace or in the chapel or garden, do not miss the opportunity to hear the "still, small voice," or the "voice of the whispering breeze" in 1 Kings 18 (also 19, if you are not going to Sinai). At the western tip of Carmel, the cloister, church, convent, and guest house for pilgrims form a complex with dramatic views over Acco, Haifa, and the Mediterranean. The Carmelite Order was founded in the prophetic spirit of Elijah by a group of Crusaders who began to live a form of religious life gathered around the chapel of Our Lady here on Mount Carmel. When the Crusader stronghold at nearby Acco (St. Jean d'Acre) fell to the Moslems in 1291, the Order migrated to Europe.

In the chapel are depictions of Elijah and Our Lady of Mount Carmel as well as St. Theresa and St. John of the Cross who restored the Order to its original contemplative charism. Saint Edith Stein, the converted Jewish philosopher who died at the hands of the Nazis, and Blessed Miriam, a Palestinian Arab who died as a young nun at the Carmel in Bethlehem are also remembered here.

BET SHEAN

The plain of Megiddo merges in the east with the Harod Valley. Near where it joins the Jordan Valley is the strategic site of Bet Shean. In the time of the Judges it was occupied by the Philistines who were able to come all the way across the country from their Pentapolis in the southwest corner on the Mediterranean coast. This was a tremendous threat to the Israelites. It was probably this very threat that forced Israel to change its political system from a confederation to a monarchy headed by the first messiah, Saul (1 Samuel). The switch was not a roaring success at first, since both Saul and his son Jonathan fell in a battle with the Philistines at nearby Mount Gilboa, and their bodies were hung from the walls of Bet Shean.

Archaeologists are still at work on this extensive site which has yielded mosaic floors and other signs of what was a very important city with a history going back five thousand years.

NAZARETH

In all the lists of cities, towns, and villages mentioned in the Old Testament, Nazareth, isolated in a detour off the trade route, does not even receive honorable mention. Recent excavation shows that there were inhabitants there during the Hebrew occupation of the land. But it was such a hick town that twelve hundred years later Nathaniel from Cana, on the main road over the hill, could ask sarcastically, "You don't expect that anything worthwhile is going to come out of Nazareth?" (John 1:46). Philip said: "Come and see for yourself." We will join them.

Basilica of the Annunciation

Basilica of Annunciation, Nazareth

The architect Muzzio (cf. plaque on inside of cortile, adjacent to the custodian's room) did this magnificent building as an offering to Mary, the Mother of God. It is a text in church history and a poem in stone based on the prologue of St. John. In this holy place, one word is added to those of the Prologue: "*Here* the Word was made flesh" (Latin: *Hic Verbum Caro factum est*), as reads the inscription in the Grotto.

The conical-shaped dome has the color of the winter tents of the Beduin which it resembles. It is inspired by the prologue of the fourth Gospel which says that he "pitched his tent among us." If you have the good fortune to be here overnight, you will see that the dome blends into the dark night sky, but the lantern it supports proclaims that the "light came into the darkness which was not able to overpower it."

There are two facades. That of the Redeemer has the words of hope addressed to Eve in Genesis, and Isaiah's Emmanuel prophecy. On the side is the facade of the Virgin setting out for the Visitation, with the words of the Salve Regina (Hail Holy Queen, Mother of Mercy, our life, our sweetness, and our hope. To thee do we cry, poor banished children of Eve. To thee do we send up our sighs, mourning and weeping in this valley of tears. Turn then, most gracious advocate, thine eyes of mercy toward us, and after this, our exile, show unto us the blessed fruit of thy womb, Jesus. O clement, O loving, O sweet virgin Mary). The bronze doors of the life of Mary in the Marian facade are the work of an American, F. Shrady.

The nations of the world were invited to contribute mosaic or tile depictions of their patronal Madonnas. Those that are not in the cortile are in the upper church. Some are inspired, some are satisfactory, some are garish, some are maudlin, and some are poor art. Something for every taste.

Upon entering the church at ground level one is immediately drawn to the baldachino over the grotto. The Annunciation took place here two thousand years ago. It was a cave house. The room built on to the front of it has disappeared (relic hunters or holy House of Loretto?). Adjacent to it is a small mosaic of a shrine built by Deacon Conon of Jerusalem, who said he was of the family of the Christ. In early Byzantine times a church was built adjacent to the grotto. The floor of the church at the top of the stairs is the level of the Crusader structure. Behind the grotto is the actual wall of the Crusader building. In the rear of the Byzantine church is the baptismal pool. The altar and pillars in front of the cave are from the seventeenth-century church built after the Franciscans had acquired the property. That church, built in haste with the sanctuary on top of the grotto, never seemed quite adequate, either for the numbers of people or for the profundity of the mystery celebrated here.

Before building the new basilica, the whole area was excavated by Fr. Bellarmino Bagatti, O.F.M., and the archaeologists from the Franciscan Biblical School in Jerusalem. Their extraordinary finds are beautifully displayed in the museum. Informative tours of the excavations and the museum are available on request in the morning, and should not be missed.

The upper church is the parish church of the Catholic Arab community of Nazareth. On Sunday mornings the Masses in Arabic, derived from the Aramaic that Jesus spoke, are joyful celebrations of the faith of those who may very well be descended from the family of Jesus. The huge mosaic in the sanctuary depicts the Constitution on the Church of Vatican II. In the floor are the coats of arms of the major councils in the history of the Church. Among the countries whose Madonnas are displayed here are France, Japan, Mexico, Poland, Canada, the United States, and over the balcony doorway, the Cubans in exile in Miami. Outside the back door, the baptistery is the gift of Germany. In the paving are the symbols of St. Francis' Canticle of the creatures.

Visit to the Basilica

Enter the cortile with its display of Marian images and the mosaic of Paul VI visiting the site in 1964, the first pope ever to do so. Both the facades and the bronze doors honoring Jesus on the front and Mary on the side are well worth a visit. Notice in the front that the Crusader basilica was about fifteen feet longer than the present one. If you are not fortunate enough to be with a group that has a liturgy scheduled, enter the lower church. The sunken area adjacent to the grotto is the Byzantine church. The grotto is open for visits only in the early morning. The baldachino is the work of an Israeli artist. The stones to the right of the grotto are the foundation of a pillar from the Crusader church. In the grotto is the inscription under the altar: *"Here the Word was made Flesh."* On the back wall the tabernacle reserves the Blessed Sacrament. The inner staircase was a late addition to provide the Crusaders access to the grotto.

The crucifix suspended over the main altar of the church is by the same Israeli artist. In the corridor adjacent to the sacristy are some interesting photos of the previous church. The oculus beneath the dome provides a sense of unity between the grotto where the Son of God came to Nazareth two thousand years ago, and the upper church where the people of Nazareth welcome him today.

Isaiah 55:6-11

Seek the Lord while you can still find him. Call upon him while he is still close to you. Let the wicked do a change of direction, and the mischievous one a change of heart. Let them turn around toward the Lord who will show his face to them, to our God who will shower his mercy upon them. "Keep in mind that my ways are not your ways, and my plans are not your plans," says your God. "As high as the heavens are above the earth, so high are my thoughts above your thoughts, my plans above your plans. For as surely as the heavens drop down their rain and snow, not to return to them until they have watered the earth and brought forth life and growth, giving both the seed that is sown and the bread from the harvest, so shall my word be that I send forth. It will not be frustrated but will do my will and bring my plan to fulfillment."

Luke 1:26-38

In the sixth month God sent the angel Gabriel to Nazareth, a town of Galilee. The angel appeared to a virgin by the name of Mary who was engaged to a man named Joseph of the family of David. "Hail Mary, full of grace, the Lord is with thee." She found this disturbing and was at a loss what to make of it. Then he said: "Don't be afraid, Mary, you are very pleasing to God, and you are going to conceive and bear a son whom you will name Jesus. He will be great and will be known as the Son of the Most High. The Lord God has prepared for him the throne of David, his ancestor. He will preside over the House of Jacob forever and there will be no end to his rule." But Mary broke in: "How can all of this possibly happen? I am still a virgin." But the angel settled it: "The Holy Spirit is resting upon you and the power of the Most High is overshadowing you. That is why your child will be called Holy. Indeed, he will be known as the Son of God."

"Besides, your cousin Elizabeth who was looked down upon because she had no children, is now six months pregnant. In her old age she is going to have a son. Why? Because nothing, absolutely nothing, is impossible with God." Mary had nothing more to say except: "Behold the handmaid of the Lord, Be it done unto me according to thy word."

Reflection

The Catholic Church now numbers over one billion people. It was not always so. In the beginning, so few accepted Jesus. The reason is simple. They were looking for something flashy, a Hollywood production. But God chose Nazareth, the prototype of the unlikely town that is the butt of every joke. Among the hicks of that backwater town he chose a young teenager who was not even married. The child that she raised here looked like every other child in town. He became like them in every way. There's the problem. He was too much like themselves, and they wanted him to be different. Look around the streets of Nazareth. You will see him in the child playing a game, the teenager chatting with friends, the young man driving the taxi. Nazareth challenges us to be open and ready for the God of surprises. *"My ways are not your ways, says the Lord."*

Prayer—The Angelus

The Angel of the Lord declared unto Mary and she conceived by the Holy Spirit. Hail Mary, full of grace . . . .

Behold the Handmaid of the Lord, be it done unto me according to thy word. Hail Mary, full of grace . . . .

*And **here** the Word was made Flesh, and dwelt among us. Hail Mary, full of grace . . . .*

Pray for us, O Holy Mother of God, that we may be made worthy of the promises of Christ.

Let us Pray: *Pour forth we beseech you, O Lord, your grace into our hearts, that we to whom the incarnation of Christ your son was made known by the message of an angel may, by his passion and cross, be brought to the glory of his resurrection through the same Christ Our Lord.*

Hymns: *O Come, O Come, Emmanuel* (page 174); *Sing of Mary* (page 168)

St. Joseph's Church

Close to the Church of the Annunciation, just past the Terra Sancta College (high school) for the boys of Nazareth is another church. Excavations indicate that it has an ancient tradition as a Holy Place. The size of the ancient cisterns in the crypt indicate that it must have been the business area of Nazareth. These two facts indicate that this was venerated because it was the business place and home of Joseph. Here the first Christian community, the first Christian family dwelt.

Matthew 1:20-23

When Jesus' Mother Mary was engaged to Joseph, but before they lived together, she was found to be pregnant by the power of the Holy Spirit. Joseph was a holy and kindly man, and did not want to embarrass her, so he was going to put her aside very quietly. But then the Lord sent his angel to him in a dream who advised him: "Joseph, Son of David, don't hesitate to bring Mary into your home. The child she carries in her womb is the gift of the Holy Spirit. She will have a boy, and you are to name him Jesus, for he will indeed save his people from their sins." This all happened because the Lord long ago had inspired a prophet to say: "Behold the Virgin shall be with child and bear a son, and they shall call him Emmanuel" which means "God is with us." Now that he understood this, Joseph woke up, got Mary, and brought her into his home.

Luke 2:48-52

When his parents returned to Jerusalem and found him amidst the scholars in the Temple, they were deeply moved. And his mother asked him, "Son, what are you up to? Your father and I have been beside ourselves trying to find you." He replied: "I wasn't lost. You must realize that I had to be in my father's house." But they still did not fully understand what was going on. He went home with them to Nazareth and obeyed them. And while he grew in wisdom and age and grace before God and his people, Mary treasured all of these things, pondering them in her heart.

Reflection

"Christian spouses, in virtue of the sacrament of matrimony, signify and partake of the mystery of that unity and fruitful love which exists between Christ and his church. Couples thereby help each other to attain to holiness in their married life and by raising and educating their children. In their state and way of life they have their own unique charism among the people of God.

From this union of Christians comes the family, from which new members of the human family are born. By the grace of the Holy Spirit received in Baptism, they are made children of God. . . . The Family is, so to speak, the domestic Church."

Vatican II, Constitution on the Church, par 11. Abbott, p. 29

Prayer

That God may pour forth his love upon our families, let us pray to the Lord. **Lord, hear our prayer.**

That from this holy place the spirit of reconciliation and forgiveness may enter into dysfunctional families, let us pray to the Lord. **Lord . . .**

For all families who are torn apart by the addictions of members, let us pray to the Lord. **Lord . . .**

For all mothers and fathers, that they may be strengthened in their vocation by the prayers of Joseph and Mary, let us pray to the Lord. **Lord . . .**

For all God's children, that they may grow in wisdom and age and grace, let us pray to the Lord. **Lord . . .**

For all families that their love may be a vibrant sign of Christ's love for the Church, let us pray to the Lord. **Lord . . .**

We come before you, Father, for from you every family in heaven and on earth takes its name. From the heavenly home that you have prepared for us, send forth your Spirit to find a home deep in our hearts. May Christ abide in us to teach us to love. May we, as members of the Church, your family on earth, be strong to grasp the breadth and height and depth of Christ's love for us which is beyond all understanding. Glory be to you whose grace is at work in us accomplishing more than we could possibly pray for or hope for. Glory be to you in Christ Jesus and the Church, now and forever. Amen (Based on Ephesians 3:14ff.).

Synagogue

It is not likely that the present building in the care of the Greek Catholic or Melkite Church is the one that Jesus preached in. But it is likely that it is built on the location of the first-century synagogue where he studied Torah and preached. It has not been excavated.

Luke 4:14-24

> Upon returning to his home town of Nazareth he went as usual to the synagogue on the sabbath. He rose up to read and was handed the scroll of Isaiah the Prophet. Unrolling the scroll, he located the passage where the prophet had written: "The Spirit of the Lord is upon me because he has anointed me. He has commissioned me to proclaim good news to the poor, liberty to captives, sight to the blind, liberation to the oppressed and to all, a year of the Lord's good will."
>
> Then he rolled up the text, returned it to the attendant, and returned to his seat. Everyone there riveted their attention on him waiting for his commentary.
>
> He said simply, "These words have come to their fulfillment even as you have been listening!"

If there are any consecrated religious, sisters, brothers, or priests here where Jesus identifies himself with the prophetic community having a mission to the marginalized, this would be an appropriate place for them to renew their vows. Even if there are no religious among the pilgrims, all could spend a few minutes praying for the religious who have touched their lives, and for vocations to the religious life.

On Religious Life in the Church

"Religious should keep in mind that through their vows they have responded to God's call to live for him alone. . . . Through their special consecration which is deeply rooted in their rebirth in Baptism, they have given themselves over totally to the work of their Lord. This brings them more deeply into the mystery of the Church, for through her they have made the offering of themselves.

"In following God, and God alone, religious in their communities should seek a happy balance of contemplation with apostolic service. By the former they are united with him in mind and heart, and by the latter they continue the work of their Redeemer in this world, establishing the Kingdom of God." (Par 5)

"May all religious spread the good news of Christ throughout the world by the witness of their faith. May that faith stir up their love for God and his people through the cross of Christ which they bear, and the hope of future glory that shines forth from their consecrated lives. Thus will their witness be seen by all and our Father in heaven will be glorified" (Par 25).

Vatican II: On Religious Life; Abbott, p. 466

Renewal of Vows

Religious: Called by God, and consecrated by the Church, I, _____ in this holy place from which my Lord Jesus Christ was sent forth, vow and promise to live in poverty because he alone is my treasure, in chastity because my heart is restless until it rests in him, in obedience because in his will is our peace.

Leader: May God who has begun this work in us in the community of his church, bring it one day to fulfillment in the community of heaven.

ENVIRONS OF NAZARETH

St. Gabriel's Church (Mary's Well)

This Greek Orthodox church is the site of Mary's Well, still a source of water. An apocryphal gospel claims that she had a preliminary vision here before the annunciation in her home. The lovely frescoed ikons, the work of the same Bulgarian artists who did the Melkite church in Jerusalem, are deteriorating due to the moisture.

School of the Adolescent Jesus

On top of the hill with a magnificent view, the Salesians do for the youth of the area what Joseph did for the adolescent Jesus. Here they learn trades that will enable them to find good jobs in Israel, so they will not be forced to emigrate to survive. The chapel with its statue of the adolescent Jesus is an oasis for prayer. Here the young people in your life can be lifted up to the Lord. The selfless and dedicated followers of Don Bosco are the professionals when it comes to putting your offerings to good use.

Monastery of the Poor Clares

This monastery, which used to be behind the wall on the main street, is now up the hill at the end of the wall, opposite the Galilee Hotel. In addition to a spectacular view over Nazareth, there is a peaceful chapel and museum of Charles de Foucald. It was here that he conceived of the Nazareth vocation of contemplation and manual labor now lived by the Little

Brothers and Sisters of Jesus. And if you want prayers, these nuns from Lebanon and France are the professionals. They live on alms and the sale of rosaries they make and lilies of the field which they mount on cards. Ask to see the olive tree in the garden planted by them on the occasion of the author's silver jubilee.

CANA

A short distance from Nazareth on the road to the Sea of Galilee is the Arab village where Jesus at the request of his mother turned the water to wine. The newly renovated "Franciscan Wedding Church" is also the parish church for the Catholic Arabs.

John 2:1-11

> On the third day a wedding took place at the village of Cana in Galilee. Jesus' mother was there. Both he and his disciples had also been invited. The host unexpectedly ran short of wine. The mother of Jesus informed him, "They have no wine." His reply to her was: "Woman, my hour has not yet come, how does their problem affect us?" His mother said to the staff, "Whatever he tells you to do, make sure you do it." For the ritual requirements of Jewish ceremonial, there were six stone water jars there. Each had a capacity of over twenty gallons. Jesus told the staff to fill them to the brim which they did. "Now have the steward test it," he said. They did exactly as they were told. The steward tested the water made wine and had not a clue as to where it had come from. But the staff knew, since they had obeyed Jesus' word. The steward checked with the groom and told him that he thought that people usually served vintage wine first and then served the common wine after the guests had been drinking a while. He was surprised that the best wine was kept until last. Jesus performed this, the first of his signs at Cana in Galilee. Thus was his glory manifested, leading his disciples to believe in him.

Reflection

The bride is never heard from; the resulting wine may have been as much as one hundred and fifty gallons; Mary is known only as Woman or Mother. Her name is never used in the entire gospel. The opening time framc tclls us that this happened on the third day, but has no reference to a first or second day. There is more here than meets the eye, much more.

The author of the gospel raises many challenges, but in the story he makes one major affirmation: Jesus chose a wedding to be the vehicle for manifesting his Divine Glory. When Paul speaks of marriage as a great sacrament and then hastens to add: "But I am speaking of this in reference to Christ and to his church," he is making the same point. Love of a married couple for each other is a song that sings to us of how Christ loves us and how we are called to love him.

Prayer for Married Couples

Father, you have given your people the blessing of marriage so that when we see a couple's love, we may learn how much you love us. Bless all married couples especially _____ and _____. May their love be a blessing upon us all. Theirs is a difficult vocation in a world that calls love what is not love. Be at their side, so that through the joy they have in each other we may find joy in you, our loving God.

That the Lord may take away the loneliness of the widowed and give their spouses rest until that day when they shall be reunited in joy, Let us pray. **Lord, hear our prayer.**

That the Lord may bless all of those whose marriages did not succeed, and give them strength and hope. Let us pray. **Lord . . .**

That the Lord may share his own love with those who are preparing for marriage, Let us pray. **Lord . . .**

That the Lord may strengthen and grace our pilgrim couples who are about to renew their marriage vows. Let us pray. **Lord . . .**

Renewal of Marriage Vows

Couples: Father, we come before you in this place made holy by Jesus and his mother. The love we have for each other in our hearts was placed there by you. You have given us as a gift to each other. Here Jesus transformed water into wine. Continue to transform us so that we may grow ever more deeply in love. May our life with each other continue to be a light that shines for all. Once again, we take each other for better for worse, for richer for poorer, in sickness and in health, until death do us part.

All: May the love of God which has been poured forth into your hearts, give hope to us who are touched by it. May the same love be with you in all of your ways and strengthen you all of your days.

Leader: May the blessing of almighty God, Father, Son, and Holy Spirit descend upon you and abide with you forever. Amen.

NAIN

The town where Jesus raised the only son of the widow is at the foot of Mount Tabor. It is one of the less frequented of the Holy Places since most pilgrims are in haste to get to Tabor or Nazareth or Tiberias. It deserves at least a nod of recognition to read the gospel account (Luke 7:11-17) and provides an opportunity to share in the prayer and sorrow of parents like this widow and Mary whose children have pre-deceased them. If the group is going to celebrate liturgy on Mount Tabor, such parents could be remembered in the prayer of the faithful.

MOUNT TABOR

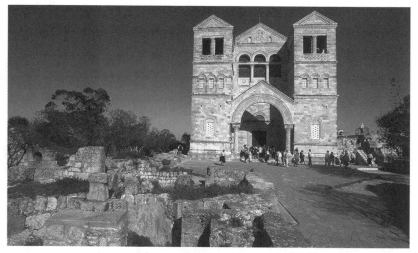

Church of Transfiguration atop Mt. Tabor, Galilee

In years gone by the standard joke was that the reason Peter, James, and John wanted to stay at the top was because they had the same taxi drivers as you have had. However, with the new road and guard rails, all of the excitement is gone. Still it can still be one of the most memorable days of a pilgrimage if it includes time for prayer, liturgy, and lunch at the pilgrims' dining room (by reservation only).

The 1900-foot-high mountain is very popular with the Israelis for scout outings, hang gliding, picnicking, etc., especially on the Sabbath (when the sanctuary is closed). In earlier days it was the object of the wrath of the prophets as a high place tempting the Israelites into the fertility cult of Baal and his wife Astarte (Judg 10:6; 2 Kings 23:13). Its earliest mention in the Hebrew Bible is the strategic battle of Mount Tabor when the prophetess and judge Deborah stirred up the Israelites to subdue the Canaanites. In Judges 4 and 5, the story is recounted in both a prose and poetic version.

For Christians however, Tabor has been identified in the Gospels with the high mountain in Galilee. Jesus' transfiguration and his great commission after the resurrection in Matthew's Gospel are celebrated here. Like the Church, the mountain is divided: the Orthodox Church of St. Elijah is to the left at the top, while the Franciscan compound of basilica, friary, retreat house, dining room (gift shop) and convent is set into the Crusader ruins along the road to the right.

The church was built by the architect Barluzzi on the foundation of the Crusader church. (You can greet him on the large rock facing the front door.) Inside stairs descend to an early Byzantine church. In the sanctuary the images of the peacocks signify glory, and the mosaics of the four angels signify the four ways in which we can still say: "We have seen his glory, the glory as of the only-begotten Son of the Father, full of grace and of truth" (John 1:14). They are in his humanity, his Real Presence, his sacrifice, and his resurrection.

Above the main sanctuary of the modern basilica is the radiant mosaic of the Transfiguration. It would have been more radiant if, after the alabaster roof was built, it did not have to be covered with lead after the first rains. The alabaster windows still give a glimpse of what might have been. In the rear, the church has accomplished what Peter, James, and John were not allowed to do: build tabernacles for Moses and Elijah.

2 Peter 1:16-19

> From Simon Peter, apostle and servant of Jesus, the Messiah. To you who know the Lord: May grace and peace overflow in your hearts.
>
> Our preaching to you about the power and the coming (Parousia) of Our Lord Jesus Christ was based neither on myth nor fable. We ourselves were there and saw his glory. He received full approbation when God the Father poured down his own honor and glory upon him and proclaimed: "This is my Son, the one whom I love, the one upon whom my favor rests." Right on this holy mountain, while we were with him, we heard that voice.
>
> Don't miss the opportunity to listen. Listen to his words and our words that come from him. They are a light guiding you in the darkness as you await the dawn when the morning star will rise in your hearts.

Matthew 17:1-8

> Jesus took Peter, James, and John and climbed with them up to the top of a high mountain so they could have some time to themselves. Right before their eyes he went through an amazing transfiguration. His face seemed to become as radiant as the sun. His clothing seemed to be transformed into light. Then both Moses and Elijah were manifested speaking to Jesus. Peter spoke and said: "Lord, how good it is for us to be here. Why don't we set up three dwelling places, one for each of you?"
>
> Even while he was speaking, they were overshadowed by a shining cloud, and from it they heard a voice: "This is my Son, the one whom I love, the one upon whom my favor rests. It is his voice that you should be listening to." The disciples didn't know what to make of this, and fell to the ground. But then it was all over, and Jesus came and put his hand on them and said: "Rise up. Be not afraid."

Reflection

Being a disciple of Jesus must have been depressing and discouraging at times. The mounting hostility, the carping criticism, and the negative attitudes must have generated a black cloud over his words and ministry. He has been accused of being an irreligious sabbath breaker. The rumor is spread that he is in the employ of Satan. The disciples hear that John the Baptist's tongue has been silenced forever.

The religious leaders claim to be the official representatives of God. They have cornered the market on his will. They occupy the chair of Moses and wear the mantle of Elijah. But there cannot be two voices that speak with authority. Since this is so, Jesus must be a fraud or a charlatan or an imposter. These are the voices that come crashing upon the disciples. They have to get away from those voices. Jesus knows it and takes them on a retreat.

They desperately needed to get away and sort things out. They had to know that they were not wrong and deluded even if the guardians of orthodox theology (Pharisees) and the Chancery Office (Sadducees) insisted they were.

On Tabor their quiet time with Jesus and the very beauty and calm of the place were so moving and inviting that they wanted to dwell there. They felt a deep reassurance when they had the vision of Jesus talking with the real religious leaders of the people, Moses, and Elijah. This was the "Good Housekeeping Seal of Approval." The invitation to hear his voice was also a warning that other voices could lead them astray. With renewed confidence they could shed their doubt, anguish and fear and just listen to him.

Tabor is a challenge to us also. We get busy and have so many voices crashing upon us with their own values, priorities, and plans. This was what led the late Joseph Cardinal Bernardin to rise early each day to spend time with Jesus. He realized that he had become so busy in the service of the Church that he had no time to be with God. **"Be still, and know that I am God!"** (Ps 46:10).

Prayer

Lord, slow us down. Sometimes we get so busy and have the news, the songs, the advertisements, the rumors, the gossip, and the nonsense challenging our values and priorities. Take us apart with your Son so that we may listen to him and not become confused, empty or hypocritical. Or worse, shallow, smug and self-righteous. Speak, Lord, we love to listen to your voice!

Matthew 28:17-20

> Jesus commissioned his disciples: "The fullness of power both in heaven and upon earth has been entrusted to me. Go out to all and make them my disciples. Baptize them in the name of the Father, and of the Son, and of the Holy Spirit. Teach them to live by all that I have commanded you. And behold I am with you always, now and forever."

Hymns: *Holy God, We Praise Thy Name* (page 162); *The King of Glory* (page 164); *Alleluia! Sing to Jesus* (page 155); *How Great Thou Art* (page 163); *Sing a New Song* (page 168); *Holy, Holy, Holy! Lord God Almighty* (page 163)

SEA OF GALILEE

Jesus spent most of his ministry around the Sea of Galilee (a.k.a.: Kineret, Tiberias, Lake of Gennesaret). Traveling the route that Jesus trod from Nazareth to Capernaum, one passes the double hillock of the Horns of Hattin where the Crusader army was defeated on July 4, 1187. On an unbearably hot day they caught sight of the water and dropped their weapons and armor and rushed to it. They were cut down by the forces of Salah ed Din (Saladin) who then went on to Nazareth, Tabor, and Jerusalem.

Events in the life of Jesus that are associated with this route are the healing of a leper (Mark 1:40-45), the disciples plucking the grain on the sabbath (Mark 2:23-28), and the parables of Matthew 13.

The lake, shaped like a harp (Hebrew: Kineret) is about twelve miles long and seven miles wide. It is the reservoir for the state of Israel and its level is dependent on the winter rains and the melting snow from Mount Hermon. During a severe drought the level was so low that the remains of a fishing boat from the time of Jesus emerged from the bottom. A wise entrepreneur has had a fleet of tourist boats modeled on it built in Alexandria, Egypt. They are known as "Jesus Boats" and ply the waters with the names Matthew, Mark, Luke, and John. The friendly and cooperative crews will raise the flag of your homeland, give a demonstration of fishing as it was done at the time of Jesus, and pause and provide a microphone so the appropriate passages may be read.

Luke 5:1-11

Jesus was on the shore, and he felt the pressure of the crowd as he was preaching. He saw two fishermen working on their nets. He got into one of their empty boats, Simon's, and asked him to pull away from the shore. He sat down and continued preaching. When he was done he asked Simon: "Can you pull out a ways and cast your nets?" Simon replied: "We can, Master, but we have been at it for the whole night and we've got nothing."

So they lowered their nets which almost broke from the number of fish they caught. They signaled to those on shore to bring the other boat, and they filled both with the catch, almost to the point of sinking. Simon Peter was ashamed and dropped to his knees saying: "Don't hang around me, Lord, I am a real sinner." Every last one of them was overwhelmed, but Jesus said: "Be not afraid, from now on you will be catching people." Without any hesitation, they steered for shore, dropped everything and followed him.

Mark 4:35-41

Another time as it grew toward evening, he said, "Set sail for the other side." They left the crowd behind, and all the boats followed the one he was sitting in. Without warning a storm raged about them, and his boat began to fill with water. He was sound asleep in the stern, and didn't stir a bit. Finally, they roused him and said: "Teacher, don't you even care that we are sinking?" Now alert, he charged the wind and the sea: "Peace. Calm down." And they did! And turning to the disciples he said: "Why are you so nervous? Don't you have any faith at all?" But they were wondering who he was that he had such power over creation.

Matthew 14:22-33

Another time, Jesus got away from the crowd and told his disciples to go ahead to the other side. He himself sought some solitude for prayer on the mountain, remaining until night drew on. The boat filled with his disciples was caught in a violent storm. In the middle of the night they caught sight of him walking on the water. They thought he was a ghost, and they were really scared and started screaming. Jesus told them to calm down. "It is I. Be not afraid."

Peter yelled to Jesus: "Lord, if that's really you out there, tell me to come to you on the water." "Come!" And Peter did just that and was doing fine until he panicked and started going down. "Jesus, Help me!" and Jesus reached out and grabbed him and said: "Why did you falter in your resolve?" As soon as both of them boarded the boat, a calm settled over the sea. His disciples did him reverence and confessed: "There is no doubt that you are the Son of God."

Hymn: *Be Not Afraid* (page 157)

The River Jordan

"There Are Two Seas"

There are two seas in Palestine. One is fresh, and fish are in it. Splashes of green adorn its banks. Trees spread their branches over it, and stretch out their thirsty roots to dip of its healing water. Along its shore the children play.

The River Jordan makes this sea with sparkling water from the hills. So it laughs in the sunshine. And men build their houses near to it, and birds their nests; and every kind of life is happier because it is there.

The River Jordan flows on south into another sea. Here is no splash of fish, no fluttering leaf, no song of birds, no children's laughter. Travelers choose another route, unless on urgent business. The air hangs above its waters and neither man nor beast nor fowl will drink. What makes this mighty difference in these neighbor seas? Not the River Jordan. It empties the same good water into both. Not the soil in which they lie; not the country round about.

This is the difference. The Sea of Galilee receives but does not keep the Jordan, for every drop that flows into it, another drop flows out. The giving and receiving go on in equal measure. The other sea is shrewder, hoarding its income jealously. It will not be tempted into any generous impulse. Every drop it gets, it keeps. The Sea of Galilee gives and lives. This other sea gives nothing. It is named the Dead.

There are two seas in Palestine. There are two kinds of people in the world. Which kind are we?

A Parable by Bruce Barton

TIBERIAS

Named after the emperor by Herod's son, Antipas, Tiberias was built as a new capital for the part of his father's kingdom that he inherited. The hot sulphur springs on the shore of the lake were and still are the attraction that directed Antipas' attention to the spot. Only John's Gospel makes any mention of it, and then only in passing (6:23). The rabbis avoided it as unclean until the destruction of Jerusalem when it became an important center of Torah study.

Its cemeteries are marked by the monuments to important religious readers. The large modern steel monument to the great Ramban (acronym for Rabbi Moses ben Maimonides), thirteenth-century author of the classic *Guide for the Perplexed* is seen on the hill on the way into town. It is a glitzy resort where miracles still happen: the Jesus boats of the pious pilgrims are changed into the waterborn discos of the pleasure seekers with the setting of the sun.

The small Church of St. Peter on the waterfront has scheduled Masses for the tourists. It also has a statue of St. Peter made from the same mold as the one in the Vatican. In the interior courtyard there is a monument recalling the Polish children saved from the Nazis and Communists who found refuge here during World War II.

CAPERNAUM

Kefer means town. The town of Naum is transliterated in several confusing ways even on the local road signs. Lectors, take courage. All of your pronunciations are correct. However Jesus pronounced it, he liked it (at least for a while. Cf. Luke 10:23-24) and the Gospels called it his own town. In one instance he is said to have gone into his house, so he may have had property here. He certainly lived here with Peter, and worshiped each sabbath in the synagogue. The walls that are seen around the site are those of the Franciscan archaeologists and have no historical significance. The red domed Church of the Greek Orthodox is a continuation of the site of the ancient city.

After the entrance (don't miss Father Martini's statue of St. Francis reaching up to Brother Sun), the large presses and mill stones indicate that it was the commercial area of town. The new church to the right, with the glass floor looking down into the excavations, shows how the house of Peter's mother-in-law developed into a synagogue church for the Jewish Christians and then into a Byzantine octagonal church. The modern Church of St. Peter has a twofold function: to protect the excavations, and to preserve them as an inviolable Holy Place. Only those with a reservation for Liturgy are permitted entrance.

The local stone is black volcanic basalt. All of the white stone lying around, much of which is beautifully carved, was brought from a distance for the building of the "white synagogue" three or four centuries after Jesus. Its beauty indicated the wealth of the town, and its carving with forbidden images indicated that the worshipers were not too orthodox. Later on, a more religious community chiseled away some of the more offensive images (e.g., Roman eagle). The foundation of the synagogue in which Jesus worshiped is clearly visible from the side of the present one. That is the one that was built for the local populace through the beneficence of a centurion whose servant Jesus cured (Luke 7:5). It was here, after the multiplication of the loaves, that he delivered the discourse on the bread of life.

John 6

> They asked him what sign he was going to perform so that they could be assured that he was worthy of their confidence. They quoted to him the precedent of the manna in the Desert from the scriptures: "He gave them bread from heaven for their food." Jesus responded, "Have no doubt about it. It was not Moses who gave it to you, but my

Father who gives you the real bread from heaven. God's bread comes down from him and is life for the world." "O, give us this bread every day," they begged. Jesus tried to make clear to them: "I myself am the bread of life" . . . They started grumbling because he claimed to be the bread of life himself . . . "Enough of your grumbling" he said, and insisted . . . "Your ancestors were indeed nourished with the manna in the desert, but where are they now? They are all dead! This is the bread that is God's gift from heaven, and whoever eats of it will never die. I myself am the living bread that has come down from heaven. If anyone eats of this bread they shall have eternal life; The bread that I will give is my flesh for the life of the world."

That set them arguing about how he could possibly give them his flesh to eat, so he insisted: "Let me tell you again and let there be no misunderstanding: If you do not eat of the flesh of the Son of Man and drink his blood, there will be no life in you. Whoever eats my flesh and drinks my blood has life unending, and I will raise them up on the last day. Whoever eats my flesh and drinks my blood abides in me, and I in them." He spoke these words in the synagogue in Capernaum.

Many of his followers said: "This is too much. He can't be serious" . . . and many of them took their leave. Jesus turned to the twelve and said, "What about you? Are you also going to leave?" Peter spoke out: "Lord, where could we possibly go, since you have the words of eternal life. We have come to believe, and now we know for sure that you are the Holy one of God."

Reflection

In the breaking of the bread, the Eucharist, we are offered life, life such as we could never have imagined or hoped for. It is the very sharing in the life of Jesus himself. And because it is the flesh and blood of the Risen Lord, it is a foretaste of our own resurrection.

The words that Jesus spoke here are the words that find their fulfillment each time we gather as a community for the breaking of the bread. We are proof that he kept his promise. Capernaum with its synagogue has fallen into ruins. His word endures forever, and because of the word he spoke here, we know that we shall live forever.

Prayer

Blessed are you Lord God, King of the universe for the Eucharist in which Christ himself is received, his sacrifice is made present, and a taste of future glory is given. Blessed be God forever.

Hymns: *I Am the Bread of Life* (page 164); *Let Us Break Bread Together* (page 165)

(Capernaum, because it was the base of operations for Jesus, presents an embarrassment of riches for the stories of his ministry. All cannot be read in situ, but at a later time you might want to reflect on: Mark 1:16-20, the call of the apostles; 1:21-28, the cure of the paralytic in the synagogue on the Sabbath; 1:29-33, the cure of Peter's mother-in-law; 2:1-12, the paralytic lowered in through the roof; 2:13-17, the call of Levi; 3:1-6, the cure in the synagogue of the man with the withered hand; 3:20-22, the accusation of insanity by his relatives; 3:23-30, the accusation of being in league with the devil; and 3:31-35, his true relatives. As a matter of fact, why not read Mark's Gospel from cover to cover. It takes less than an hour. A pilgrimage should leave one hungry for the word of God.)

TABGHA

The name of this spot is the corruption of the Greek for "seven springs." You see the water from them in the conduit along the highway. They are salty and are not allowed to flow into the sweet water of the Sea of Galilee. This is the site of the Primacy of Peter in John's Gospel and the multiplication of the loaves and fishes in the Synoptics.

Church of the Primacy

John 21:1-17

> At the sea of Tiberias, Jesus again appeared to his disciples.
> . . . Peter was among them and said he was going fishing, so some of the others decided to join him. By the time the sun rose, they still had caught nothing. Then Jesus appeared on the shore but they did not recognize him. He called: "Children, how's the fishing?" They replied that they had not caught a thing. He called back that if they cast the net on the other side they would catch something. They did, and caught so many that they couldn't haul the net into the boat.
> Finally recognizing that it was the Lord because the beloved disciple had told him . . . Simon Peter jumped into the water while the others followed towing the nets . . . Jesus invited them to broil some of the fish they had caught on the charcoal fire where he was already cooking some bread and fish. . . . Then he served them breakfast.

When they had finished, he said to Simon Peter, "Simon, Son of John, do you love me more than these?" "Yes, Lord, you know that I love you." Jesus said, "Feed my lambs." A second time Jesus said, "Simon, Son of John, do you love me?" "Yes, Lord, you know that I love you." Jesus asked a third time, even though Peter was losing patience. "Simon, Son of John, do you love me?" "Lord, you know everything, you know that I love you." Jesus said, "Feed my sheep."

Reflection

Each of the evangelists is convinced that Peter was given a special role in the Church, but each tells the story differently. In Mark it is a simple change of name. In Luke it is Jesus praying for Peter at the Last Supper that he may be able to strengthen the community. In Matthew it is the conferral of the keys at Caesarea Philippi. Details may differ but there is no doubt that the role of "universal pastor" must have been intended by Jesus. Catholics rejoice in this and regard it as a special token of Jesus' concern for the flock. This is beautifully illustrated by the bronze statue of Jesus handing the shepherd's staff to Peter (the last work that the late Fr. Andrea Martini, O.F.M., created for the Holy Places). If the pilgrimage has had a strong spiritual element that would qualify it as a retreat, then the priest-director may impart the Papal blessing. Otherwise someone in the group may invoke the following blessing based on Hebrews 13:20ff.:

Blessing Prayer

May the God of peace who raised up from the dead the great shepherd of the sheep, Jesus the Lord, sustain, bless and guide his vicar, our Universal Pastor _____. To him has been committed the care of the flock. Perfect him, Father, in holiness and guide him to do your will. In all things may he strive that your kingdom may come and that your will may be done. To your Son, Jesus the Lord, the good shepherd of our souls, be power, honor, blessing, and glory forever and ever. Amen.

Hymns: *Like a Shepherd* (page 166); *The Church's One Foundation* (page 158)

Church of the Multiplication

The new church of the Benedictines is built to the specifications of the one built here in 450. That was built in such a way that the altar was above the "Mensa Christi," the rock that came to be known as the "Dining Table of Christ" from which he fed the crowd.

In the forecourt are millstones on the shore of the sea that vividly illustrate Jesus' words: "Woe to you who scandalize one of these little ones. It were better for you to have a millstone tied around your neck and to be thrown into the depths of the sea" (Matt 18:6).

Mosaic detail: Miracle of loaves and fishes, Tabgha Church

The atrium contains a baptismal pool. Much of the floor of the church is the original fifth-century mosaic with flora and fauna that are more at home on the Nile than the Jordan, indicating the origin of the artist. At the Mensa Christi is one of the most famous mosaics in the world: the loaves and fishes, over fifteen hundred years old.

Mark 6:30-44

> When the apostles returned from their missionary journey, Jesus suggested that they come apart and refresh themselves. People were so demanding on them that they hardly had a chance to eat. They got into a boat to get away to a quiet place, but some people saw what they were up to and spread the word. They were at the quiet place even before the boat touched shore. By the time Jesus disembarked the crowd was huge. His heart went out to them because they were like sheep, meandering around without a shepherd to care for them. He tried to satisfy their hunger for the word of God. By

the time he finished, it was pretty late, and his disciples suggested that Jesus dismiss them to go off and see if they could get something to eat. "You give them something to eat," he said. Confused, they asked him if they were supposed to spend a half year's wages just for bread. He ignored them and told them to find out how many loaves there were. They reported back that they could get together only five loaves and two fish. He told them to arrange the people on the grass into groups.

Then Jesus took the five loaves and two fish in his hands, lifted his eyes to heaven, blessed them and broke the bread and gave it to the disciples to share with the crowd. He divided the two fish among them also and then when all were satisfied they gathered up the leftovers into twelve wicker baskets. Over five thousand people had been fed!

Reflection

What a strange thing for Jesus to say: "You give them something to eat." He knew as well as the disciples that they had nothing to offer the people. It almost seems as if he is playing a game with them. "You, from your own resources, try solving the problem. See how far you get under your own power." That could only lead to a sense of frustration and helplessness on the part of the disciples. That was a good place for them to be. It brought them to their knees and made them realize that if they were going to be effective, it would not be from their own resources but because of the power of Jesus within them. Through frustration he brought them to a deeper faith, knowing that without him their efforts were futile. So are ours! "I am the vine, you are the branches. Whoever abides in me, and I in them bears much fruit, for apart from me you can do nothing" (John 15:5).

Prayer

O thou who clothest the lilies, and feedest the birds of the air; who leadest the lambs to pasture, and the hart to the water's side; who multiplied loaves and fishes, and converted the water to wine. Do thou come to our table as giver and guest to dine.

Hymns: *You Satisfy the Hungry Heart* (page 171); *Let Us Break Bread Together* (page 165); *Like a Shepherd* (page 166)

MOUNT OF BEATITUDES

Church of the Beatitudes above the Sea of Galilee

Matthew says the Sermon was on the Mount; Luke says it was on the Plain. They are both right. The evangelists have compiled words that are précis of many of Jesus' sermons in many places. This mount is likely one of those places. If not, it is so lovely it should be! Matthew intended all of Jesus' words in chapters seven and eight to be listened to in one sitting. It is a blessing if you can find a quiet place and do so. The Beatitudes themselves, the Magna Carta of Christianity, are so familiar that they can lose their impact. The following paraphrase is offered to provide new insights into old truths. Each beatitude is followed by a quote to further illustrate it. To better appreciate the insight the traditional form of each beatitude may be read, followed with the paraphrase and quote.

Matthew 5:3-11

Blessed are the poor in Spirit.
Blessed are the sorrowful.
Blessed are the meek.
Blessed are they who hunger and thirst for righteousness.
Blessed are the merciful.
Blessed are the pure of heart.
Blessed are the peacemakers.
Blessed are those who are victims for the cause of justice.

You delight me when there is room only for me in your heart!
[All I want is to know Christ Jesus.]
You delight me when you are disturbed because I am not loved!
[Come to me all you who labor and are heavily burdened.]
You delight me when you are at peace, knowing that I am your Abba!
[Be still and know that I am God.]
You delight me when you yearn for me more than for food and drink!
[Whether you eat or drink, do all for the glory of God.]
You delight me when you are an instrument of my loving kindness!
[Forgive us our trespasses as we forgive those who trespass against us.]
You delight me when you have a one-track mind, and it is on me!
[Our hearts are restless until they rest in you.]
You delight me when your life means peace and fulness of life for others!
[My peace I leave with you. As the Father has sent me, so do I send you.]
**You delight me when you bear my cross for it leads to the fulness of life
with me.**
*[Eye has not seen, nor ear heard what God has prepared for those who
love him.]*
What will separate us from the love of Christ?
Will anguish or distress or persecution?
Will famine or nakedness or peril or the sword?
I am convinced that neither death nor life, nor angels nor principalities,
Nothing in the present or in the future, or in the heights or in the depths,
Nothing, nothing at all, will be able to separate us from the love of God,
Which is his gift to us in Christ Jesus, Our Lord.

Hymns: *Be Not Afraid* (vs. 3; page 157); *Peace Prayer of St. Francis*
(page 167); *Sing to the Mountains* (page 169); *How Great Thou Art* (all
verses; page 163)

BAPTISM IN THE JORDAN RIVER

The very beautiful spot where the waters of the sea of Galilee flow into
the Jordan River has been improved by a kibbutz for the accommodation of
Christians. You will actually be renewing your baptismal commitment on a
kibbutz! The Gospels are neither clear nor in agreement where John was
preaching and Jesus was baptized. If you eavesdrop on the fundamentalists
who frequent this spot, you will hear some bizarre sacramental theology.

We come here to renew, to reaffirm, and to say yes to the new life in
Jesus into which we were born again when our godparents spoke on our

behalf at our baptism. The ceremony of renewal, as with that of the sacrament of baptism, may be by immersion in the water, being sprinkled with water, or having it poured over your head.

Mark 1:1-11

> Here begins the Gospel of Jesus Christ, the Son of God, the prophet Isaiah set the tone for it in his proclamation: My herald will go before you; he will make sure that the way is ready for you. His voice is the one that proclaims in the desert: "Prepare the way of the Lord, make straight his paths."
>
> John the Baptist came forth, urging people to repent and be baptized as a sign that their sins were forgiven. . . . However, he was careful to let them know: "The one who is to come has the real power . . . I am not even worthy to kneel down to him, while loosening the strap of his sandals. My baptism has been with water. His baptism will be with the Holy Spirit!"
>
> It was at that time that Jesus came from Nazareth of Galilee and was baptized in the Jordan by John. As he rose up out of the water, he saw the heavens opening up and the Spirit in the form of a dove coming upon himself. And there was a voice that came forth from the heavens: "You are my beloved Son. I am well pleased with you."

Celebration of Baptismal Renewal

You must be conscious of the fact that every one of us who was baptized in Christ Jesus was baptized into his death, so that as surely as he was raised from death by the glorious power of the Father, we might walk in newness of life.

At these sacred waters in which your Lord and Savior Jesus Christ was baptized:

Will you continue to confess that Jesus is Lord, both by your word and your life? **We will.**

Will you continue to live the Holy Gospel, and be a light to the world? **We will.**

Since in baptism you have risen with Christ, will you continue to seek the things that are above? **We will.**

Do you believe in God, the Father almighty, the creator of heaven and earth? **We do.**

Do you believe in his Son, born of the Virgin Mary who gave himself for you? **We do.**

Do you believe in the Holy Spirit, the Lord and giver of life, who dwells in you? **We do.**

Because of the Holy Spirit who has been poured forth in our hearts, we are no longer slaves but children of God and can sing: *Our Father, who art in heaven . . .*

(Sprinkling of water from the Jordan)

Hymns: *Abba! Father!* (page 155); *Battle Hymn of the Republic* (vs. 2: In the beauty of the lilies; page 157)

CAESAREA PHILIPPI (BANIAS)

A ride up over the Golan Heights with a view into Syria and the cross-roads of the ancient world to the foot of Mount Hermon is a pleasant way to get away from twentieth-century civilization and experience the land as it was in the time of Jesus. The route passes through the Druse villages and offers a spectacular view of the Crusader fortress of Nimrud on the way to Herod Philip's capital of Caesarea Philippi. Ongoing excavations show a remarkable religious and political hub for northern Galilee where the source of the River Jordan used to flow dramatically out of a huge cave at the foot of Mount Hermon.

Greeks and Romans saw the exuberance of nature, and declared it to be the kingdom of Pan, which provided the name it bears today, Banias. The Psalmist saw it and proclaimed it the kingdom of Yahweh: "The heavens and the earth you alone brought to be. Without you there is no north or south, and so both Tabor and Hermon join in the praise of your name" (Ps 89:12). Jesus saw the source of the life-giving Jordan bursting from the massive rock and was reminded of the rock upon which he would build his church. And that Rock would be responsible for the keys of another Kingdom.

Matthew 16:16-23

> Upon coming to Caesarea Philippi, Jesus asked his disciples what they were hearing about who he was. They answered that people were confused about his identity, some claiming that he was John the Bap-tist, others that he was Elijah, and still others suspected him of being Jeremiah, or at least another of the prophets. "And what conclusion have you come to about me?" Jesus asked. Simon Peter jumped in and said: "You are the Messiah, the Son of the living God." "How blessed are you, Simon, son of Jonah because what you just said

came not from any human opinion, but by a revelation from my heavenly father."

"Now listen to what I say: You are Peter, the Rock, and on this Rock I will build my church, and the powers of hell will stand helpless before it. I will give you the keys to the Kingdom of heaven. Whatever you bind on earth will be bound in heaven, and whatever you loose on earth shall be loosed in heaven." Then he forbade his disciples to let anyone know that he was the messiah.

He started to reveal to his disciples that his future in Jerusalem would be one of suffering and death at the hands of the authorities, but he would rise again. Then Peter got him alone and said, "God help us, Lord, we'll make sure that you won't have to go through that." Jesus faced up to Peter and let him have it: "Out of my sight! You are a Satan! You are in my way! What you are saying now is not God's plan for me. It is a merely human way of looking at my future."

Reflection

Jesus' use of the analogy of a solid foundation on the "Rock" easily leads people to think of the Church as a structure or institution. Even Francis of Assisi fell into that error. When the voice from the Crucifix of San Damiano sent him to "Rebuild my church, for it is falling into ruin," he ran around begging stones and mortar. A major manifestation of the "edifice complex"! The Church is (without excluding structure or institution) community. It is the people of God. It is the Body of Christ. Institutions are at their best when they are efficient. A community is at its best when it is filled with love. Institutions are supposed to put out a good product. A community (like the family) is supposed to nourish and guide its members to maturity. The Church is both institution and community. But when its members have to go outside the institution to find a sense of community there is something wrong with its priorities.

Immediately after the conferral of the keys, Jesus had to correct Peter's priorities about himself. Paul VI reminded us that this is an ongoing process for the Church as well:

"The church is an evangelizer, but she begins by being evangelized. She is the community of believers, the community of hope lived and communicated, the community of love; and she needs to listen unceasingly to what she must believe, to her reasons for hoping, to the new commandment of love. She is the people of God, immersed in the world, and often tempted by idols."

"Evangelii Nuntiandi #15"
Daughters of St. Paul

Most Rev. J. Terry Steib, S.V.D., bishop of Memphis, first shared the following meditation at the National Congress of Black Catholics:

For a world full of sin . . . we need a church full of holiness.
For a world that's going down . . . we need a church that's going up.
For a world filled with hell . . . we need a church filled with heaven.
For a world that's out of tune . . . we need a church that is in harmony.
For a world full of war . . . we need a church that's full of peace.
For a world full of crime . . . we need a church that's full of honesty.
For a world full of defeat . . . we need a church that's full of victory.
For a world full of "bad news" . . . we need a church that's full of "good news."
For a world that believes in "playing" . . . we need a church committed to praying.
For a discouraged world . . . we need an encouraged church.
In a world at its worst . . . we need a church at its best.

THE MEDITERRANEAN COAST

This guide is primarily concerned with the Holy Places important to the life and ministry of Jesus. With the sole exception of the healing of the Canaanite woman's daughter near Sidon, now in S. Lebanon, we are not aware that he spent any time on the Mediterranean coast. Yet, some places there are worth a visit because of their strategic role in the history of the Church. If you felt paralyzed when you arrived at Lod's Ben Gurion Airport after a very long flight, you were in good company. Lod is ancient Lydda of Acts 9:32 where Peter raised up the paralytic.

The Prince of the Apostles then went on to Jaffa (of which Tel Aviv was built a century ago as a suburb!) where he stayed at the house of Simon the tanner. Here he cured Tabitha (Acts 9:36ff.) and had the vision on the roof leading him to open the Church to the Gentiles. This he did by going to Caesarea Maritima and bringing Cornelius and his family to Jesus. Thus, it is the birth place of the Gentile Church.

Here, in secondary usage was found the Pontius Pilate inscription being used as a seat in the theater. Paul spent two years in prison here (Acts 23:31ff.) before appealing to Caesar and being sent to Rome. After the destruction of Jerusalem, Caesarea became a great center of the early Church with a library rivaling the famed one of Alexandria, and a school of scribes that assured the spread of the good news.

WHAT'S NEXT?

Now you know why the Book of Revelation describes heaven as the new Jerusalem. If your earthly pilgrimage has been a joy, remember that *"eye has not seen nor ear heard, nor has it entered into the human heart to imagine what God has prepared for those who love him"* (1 Corinthians 9). After this, there's only heaven. (But come back again, if God so wills. Once is not enough!)

If you want to spend more time in prayer, the Trappists in Latroun have a guest house, the Sisters of St. Joseph have a splendid retreat house: Our Lady, Ark of the Covenant in Abu Ghosh. The Franciscans have hermitages in the Garden of Gethsemane and facilities for retreats on Mount Tabor. Or you could spend time adjacent to the shrines at the very reasonable and comfortable Casa Novas run by the Friars in Jerusalem, Bethlehem, and Nazareth.

Prayer at the End of the Pilgrimage

Father, we have walked in the steps of your Son. We have seen the lilies of the field. We have heard the birds of the air: he said that both of them tell of your concern. We have been warmed by the sun that shone on him, cooled by the breezes that refreshed him. We have been to the sea where he calmed the storm; to the waters where your Spirit came upon him. We have sorrowed at Calvary . . . but we rejoiced at the empty tomb, for the same power by which he was raised is now at work in us who believe.

Bless all Palestinians and Israelis who have welcomed us to their homeland. Protect and strengthen our Christian brothers and sisters who dwell here. Let your justice and peace prevail throughout the land. Bring us all one day to the heavenly Jerusalem to shout our Alleluias forever.

Appendices and Index

Appendix I

GOSPEL

A pilgrimage is a means of following the gospel. This is not because the four written Gospels indicate clearly the geographical locations in the life of Jesus, as if they were composed to be accurate biographies. They were written to be expansions and amplifications of the words of Jesus, "Come follow me." His invitation was never meant to call us to visit the places made holy by his presence. They are an invitation to enter into his holiness.

Matthew, Mark, Luke, and John never thought they were providing us with a road map to the Holy Land. They did think they were extending to us the same invitation which they had received. A pilgrimage to the land that is called "holy" because of him is just one more way of saying yes to his invitation.

The Gospels are good news, but not because they satisfy our curiosity as to the where and when in the life of Jesus. They are sparse in biographical details. That was not a preoccupation of the evangelists. They are good news because they are interested in helping us to change our biographies, so that Jesus might be Lord of our life.

In 1964 Pope Paul VI directed his Pontifical Biblical Commission to publish a decree on the nature of the Gospels so that we might benefit as much as possible in reading and praying them. It said that we "must take careful note of the three stages of tradition by which the teaching and the life of Jesus have come down to us."

The first stage is the teaching and activity of Jesus during his lifetime. This stage shows that he was preoccupied in word and miracle with only one thing, the Kingdom of God, which is the same as his own Lordship over the lives of others. He invited all to find the center of gravity of their lives in himself. Basic to this first stage is the realization of his humanity. "He became like us in everything except sin" (Heb 4:15). Intrinsic to this is his Jewishness. In the state of Israel, the homeland of the Jewish people and a significant part of the Holy Land, that fact is vividly brought into focus. As pilgrims travel about that country and the Palestinian territories, they should be more and more aware that the Kingdom of God is not a place to be visited, but the power of God in their lives. Likewise, they should grasp the opportunity in their contacts with the Semitic (Arab and Jew) inhabitants to get to know what Jesus was like.

The second stage in the formation of the Gospels, according to the decree of the Pontifical Biblical Commission, is after the resurrection and ascension of Jesus. Then the Church remembered, meditated upon, and proclaimed the Good News. In their eucharistic gatherings, faced with the challenge of how to live life with Jesus, they pondered what he had said and done and adapted the sayings and events of his life to their needs. This first gospel was oral, as Paul indicates when he writes the first Christian document to the Thessalonians about the year A.D. 50: "The Gospel that I brought to you was not just words, it was in part grace, in part the Holy Spirit, and in part my own enthusiastic faith" (1:5). A pilgrimage in the footsteps of Jesus is at the same time a pilgrimage to the life setting of the first Christian communities. It is an opportunity to do what they did: remember the stories and sayings of Jesus and find your identity in him.

The third stage eventuates in the written Gospels as we know them today. It is the stage of the evangelists Matthew, Mark, Luke, and John. Three significant happenings resulted in the need to have a written record of what to then had been mostly oral tradition. The first is a non-happening: the second coming (Parousia) of Jesus did not occur in their lifetime as the first generation of Christians thought it would. Secondly, those who had been witnesses to him were dying off. Finally, the destruction of Jerusalem and the Temple in the year 70 forced them into an identity crisis and they had to ask essential questions about their relationship with the religion of Jesus, Judaism.

Around the time of the destruction of Jerusalem, Mark was the first one to produce a gospel. He was followed by Luke and Matthew, who recognized Mark's contribution, and borrowed from him, but felt that the unique situations and problems of their own communities demanded their own gospels. Toward the end of the century John's masterpiece reached its final form. Thus each of the four pastors of diverse and varied parishes gathered the written and oral materials that had been handed on to them, and produced their invitations to life with Christ, and how to live it. Each gospel reflects the point of view and needs of both the author and the community for which he wrote it.

As the Vatican document puts it: "The sacred authors for the benefit of the churches, took this earliest body of instruction, which had been handed on orally at first and then in writing . . . and set it down in the four Gospels. In doing this, each of them followed a method suitable to the special purpose which he had in view. They selected certain things out of the many which had been handed on; some they synthesized, some they explained with an eye to the situation of the churches, painstakingly using every means of bringing home to their readers the solid truth of the things in which they had been instructed. For, out of the material which they had received, the sacred authors selected especially those items which were adapted to the varied circumstances and with that end. And since the meaning of a statement depends, amongst other things, on the place which it has in a given sequence, the evangelists, in handing on the words or the deeds of our Savior, explained them for the advantage of their readers by respectively setting them, one evangelist in one context, another in another."

This third stage has several implications. First, there will be differences in the contexts of time and place in which the evangelists arrange the events in the life of Jesus. Matthew asserts that Jesus preached the "Sermon on the Mount" while Luke has it on the plain. The Synoptics (Matthew, Mark, and Luke) have Jesus cleansing the Temple at the end of his life while John places it at the beginning. The authors themselves were conscious of these variations and the readers must ask themselves what they intended by them. For example, Jesus is the new Moses in Matthew's portrayal. Like Moses of old, he must impart God's will from a mountain, thus the "Sermon on the Mount." Far from confusing, these variations give rich insights into the person and meaning of Jesus.

The context, too, into which the author inserts his material also provides insights. A comparison shows that only Luke places the account of the ambition of the apostles at the Last Supper. His contrast of the institution of the Eucharist in which Jesus gives, and the attitude of his followers who want to grab, is startling, as Luke intended it to be.

In the early Church a man named Tatian, misunderstanding the genius and gifts which each evangelist shares, thought that their differences and variations were confusing. He tried to popularize his "Diatesseron" ("One out of Four"), an effort that, if successful, would have deprived us of the rich theologies and spiritualities of Matthew, Mark, Luke, and John. The existence of four and not just one gospel shows us how rich and varied can be the manifestation of the person of Jesus. As a matter of fact, it can be a challenge for each of us to become an evangelist. As one banner proclaimed: "The only Gospel some people may ever read is the one that you write with your life."

The rich and varied manifestation of the person of Jesus in the four Gospels should remind us that they also manifest the rich and diverse varieties of life in the early Church. Perhaps in no other city in the world has that tradition been preserved as vibrantly as it has in Jerusalem. If one can ignore the competition which is un-Christian and participate in the variety of life and ritual which celebrates Christ in his Church, the faith and vision of the pilgrim can be greatly enriched. Jerusalem is like a new Pentecost in which Greeks, Latins, Syrians, Armenians, Coptics, Ethiopians, and Russians, to mention a few, all hear and proclaim the mystery of Christ in their own way (Acts 2:11). If each pilgrim does the same, then the pilgrimage will have been successful, and the gospel will become again what it was in the beginning: the living, vibrant proclamation that Jesus is Lord and he invites us to share his life.

Appendix II

PEOPLES OF THE HOLY LAND

Arabs

Originally this was the designation of the peoples, mostly Bedouin, of the Arabian peninsula, who spoke the Semitic language that came to be called Arabic. Most of them adopted the religion of Islam whose book of revelation, the Koran, was written in Arabic. Those who embraced the religion had to learn Arabic in order to read their holy book. Because they spoke the language, they, too, came to be known as Arabs, for example, the Egyptians.

Armenians

Armenians, peoples from around the Caspian Sea, partly in Turkey, and partly in Russia, were the first as a nation to embrace Christianity in the third century. They quickly established themselves in Jerusalem where they formed a monastic community to assist pilgrims. They settled in the quarter of the city now named after them, where the tomb of St. James, the first bishop of Jerusalem is found, and his successor, the Armenian patriarch lives. The population was greatly expanded when many fled to Jerusalem during the Turkish persecution of 1915. Admission to the Armenian quarter is limited to visits to their museum and for vespers in their cathedral at three o'clock each afternoon. Their clergy can be recognized by their peaked hoods. Some are in union with the Pope (Third Station). The main body of them are known as the Armenian Apostolic (not orthodox) Church.

Bedouin

Bedouin are members of nomadic tribes who wander through the Arabian peninsula, the Sinai, and Palestine. They move with the seasons and their life-support is their flocks. They have their own culture, customs, law, and are Moslem, according to their own interpretation. They freely move across national boundaries, but are being hemmed in as "civilization" encroaches upon their traditional lands. Many have pitched their tents along the sides of the wadis between Jerusalem and Jericho.

Copts

The word is derived from Egyptian. Today it designates Christian Egyptians, the only ones who use the ancient language: Coptic. They have their own ritual, liturgy, hierarchy, and pope. Pope Paul VI and Pope Shenouda affirmed their belief in the same creed, signaling that there is no break (schism) between them. Monasticism in the Church originated among the Copts, and they have been present in Jerusalem for centuries.

Druse

The Druse comprise a sect of the Moslems whose beliefs and practices have until now been clouded in mystery. It is known that they expect a mahdi (messiah) who will be born of a male. Older males wear baggy black trousers, with a slit, in case they should be chosen to be the instrument of the holy one's appearance. They also venerate Jethro, the father-in-law of Moses, and gather annually to honor him. Shunned by orthodox Moslems, those who dwell on Mount Carmel welcomed the establishment of the state of Israel and have served with distinction in the IDF (Israel Defense Forces). However, those who found themselves in occupied territory at the foot of Mount Hermon after the 1967 war have remained loyal to the Syrians. To show this, they cast their ballots over the fortified border by loud speaker, facing Damascus.

Ethiopians

Christianity in Ethiopia is traced back to the baptism of the Ambassador of Queen Candace by the deacon Philip in a river near Gaza (Acts 8:26ff.). In Jerusalem some of the community live in huts on the roof of the chapel of St. Helena of the Holy Sepulcher. Dignified and gracious, they are welcoming of visitors. The Uniate Ethiopians are the only group to have their seminary inside the Vatican.

Ethiopian Jews

The visitor to Israel may be startled to see black soldiers in the IDF or black men wearing yarmulkas. However, the Queen's ambassador in the above passage is a Jew who had come to Jerusalem to worship and was reading Isaiah when he encountered Philip. According to legend, the Jews of Ethiopia trace their lineage back to Solomon and the Queen of Ethiopia. They claim to be descendants of the tribe of Dan, some of whom fled the Assyrians at the destruction of Samaria in 721 (not so preposterous if the Mormons can believe that all ten tribes fled to America and became the American Indians!). They were brought to Israel in a major airlift and given citizenship as immigrant Jews. However, they are technically not Jews (of the tribe of Judah), but Danites (of the tribe of Dan). This is a source of friction in the Israeli religious community.

Franciscans

Francis of Assisi (1181–1226) visited the Holy Land in 1219 and left some brothers of his newly founded Order of Friars Minor to live a Christian presence among the Moslems. Crusader religious were also knights and were forced out in 1187. The friars filled the vacuum, eventually being appointed official custodians of the Holy Places. For this reason they are known as the Custody of the Holy Land and their superior as the Father Custos. Since the Latin Patriarch of Jerusalem had to flee with the Crusaders, leaving the Holy Land without a Latin bishop, the Custos, to this day uses miter and crosier when he celebrates in the shrines. Until the re-establishment of the Latin Patriarchate in 1848, the friars of the custody were the only ones who cared for the pastoral needs of not only the pilgrims, but also of the Latin Catholic population, with parishes, schools, hospitals, clinics, orphanages, etc. At the first station, "The Flagellation" on the Via Dolorosa, they staff a Biblical School, some of whose professors have a well-deserved reputation for their excavations at the Herodian, the Mount of Olives, Nazareth, and Capernaum, among other digs.

Franks

Since a large proportion of the Crusaders came from France, and the kings and patriarchs of Jerusalem came from their number, to this day members of the Western or Latin Church are sometimes referred to as "Franks."

Jews

The children of Abraham descended from his great grandson, Judah (except those named Cohen or Levi, who descended from the tribe of Levi). Even if they might be descended from another tribe (Paul claimed the tribe of Benjamin [cf. Phil 3:5]) they are still referred to as Jews.

After the fall of Jerusalem in A.D. 70 most of them joined their kin who had already settled in the major cities of the Roman Empire (The Diaspora). Those who settled in central or eastern Europe spoke Yiddish and were called Ashkenazi (Heb. Ashkenaz = Germany). Those who found refuge in Spain spoke Ladino and were called Sephardic (Heb. Sephard = Spain). These latter were expelled in 1492 and found homes in the Ottoman Empire (Greece, Turkey, Mid-East, and North Africa). In Israel their diversity is highlighted by the fact that both groups have their own state-recognized chief rabbi.

Those European Jews who felt that it was necessary to live by themselves (ghettos) in order to observe the Law faithfully and to preserve their culture and customs, became known as Orthodox. Many became so attached to their village rabbi (*rebbe* or *reb*) of two or three centuries ago, that they preserve not only his teaching, but also his clothing. Notice the varieties, including fur hats, satin coats, white caftans, knickers, fringes of prayer shawls, etc. The basic Orthodox dress is black fedora and suit with white shirt and no tie. The women, however, dress in vivid colors and patterns, but must shave their heads upon marriage, and henceforth cover their heads with a wig or kerchief.

One group revolted against what they perceived as the oppressive and negative legalism of the rabbis of their time, and burst forth in a spontaneous and joyful expression of how to live out God's liberating love (Hesed) and became known as Hassidim (cf., *Fiddler on the Roof*).

Others assimilated into the culture of their host nation and in the process saw their Judaism as ethnic and not religious. Many, however, especially those who migrated to the United States, tried to retain a religious dimension adapted to the modern world, and established the Conservative and Reform Movements. The Orthodox community in Israel see them as totally casting aside their Jewishness, and have led the fight against them with the perennial battle in the Knesset on "Who is a Jew?"

The highly personal, vicious, and vitriolic criticisms of the teaching of one rabbi and his disciples against the teachings of another are aired in public and are an embarrassment to non-religious Jews. However, for Christians they help put in context what may appear to be un-Christian or even anti-

Semitic accusations against the Jews and particularly the Pharisees in the New Testament. Often it is just another manifestation of rabbinic rivalry.

An observant religious male of whatever persuasion can be recognized by his wearing of the Yarmulka or Kipa (but don't confuse a Friar with his brown or black "Soli Deo" or a Catholic bishop with his purple zuchetto with an observant Jew!).

Melkites

The Semitic word for king or emperor is melek and so those Eastern Christians who adhered to the orthodox faith of the emperor in Constantinople came to be known as Melkites. They are uniates, i.e., in union with the pope. But, as a branch of the Eastern or Oriental Church, they have their own patriarch in Damascus and their own rite in the celebration of the Liturgy. They have their headquarters in Jerusalem at the second left inside Jaffa Gate. Sharing in the celebration of their liturgy on Sunday morning is literally a little bit of heaven. If that is not possible, at least visit and pray in their church, frescoed with beautiful icons. The one by the rear door of Peter and Andrew embracing celebrates the embrace of Paul VI, patriarch of Rome, and Athenagoras, patriarch of Istanbul on the Mount of Olives in 1964, lifting the mutual excommunications of 1054. The main entrance to the church is closed except on Sundays but admission may be gained by request through their pilgrim hotel around the corner.

Maronites

Lebanese Christians who are all in union with Rome are called Maronites. Their liturgy, ritual, and customs date from the monastic community founded by St. Maron (d. 410). They have their own patriarch, and like all uniates the period after Vatican Council II has found them reclaiming their Eastern heritage after centuries of "Latinization" by Rome. In Jerusalem they are located behind the Christian Information Center at Jaffa Gate where the Sisters of St. Therese operate a charming and small pilgrims hotel with a beautiful chapel and roof garden.

Moslems

Moslems follow the teachings of the prophet Mohammed (d. 632) in seeking the will of God. (Islam = submission) as found in the Koran. The prophet sought to convert the polytheist Bedouin of the Arabian Peninsula to monotheism. He respected the "People of the Book," Christians and Jews. The Moslems trace their descent from Abraham through Ishmael and have great respect and affection for the prophet Jesus (Nebi Issa) and his mother the Lady Miriam. Conversion to Islam involves simply the confession that there is no God but Allah (the Arabic word for God, used also by Christian Arabs).

The observant Moslem must adhere to the five pillars:

1. There is no God but Allah, and Mohammed is his prophet.
2. This is to be acknowledged in prayer five times a day.
3. A tithe is reserved from one's income for the needy.
4. A total fast must be observed during the Lunar month of Ramadan.
5. During one's lifetime a pilgrimage should be made to Mecca, Medina, and Jerusalem (called 'el Quds, *the* Holy).

There is no priesthood, ritual, or sacrifice. It is a religion of the word, proclaimed and prayed. It has no inherent antagonism to Christianity. Bad feelings arose when the Crusaders slaughtered every man, woman, and child in Jerusalem in 1099. A careful study of the history of Judaism and Christianity will reveal that Islam has not cornered the market on fanaticism or terrorism.

In Jerusalem the Dome of the Rock, now the most visible building in the skyline marks the spot where legend has it that Mohammed came on a midnight journey from Mecca, to be caught up into the mysteries of the seventh heaven, returning the same night.

Orthodox

Capitalized and used in the context of the East, for Christians the word Orthodox means only the Greek Orthodox Church, which claims to have preserved "right faith" or orthodoxy. Like the empire, it was centered in Constantinople or Byzantium. The Byzantine Empire disappeared with the fall of the city to the Turks, but the Ecumenical Patriarch retains his headquarters there. He is first in honor, but all other national churches in union with him have their own patriarch as does the Orthodox Church of Jerusalem. The title of Orthodox is claimed by many other independent national (autocephalous) churches such as the Russian, Bulgarian, etc.

Since only the celibate clergy can become bishops and hence patriarch, the choice usually devolves upon the monks. In Jerusalem they live as the "Brotherhood of the Holy Sepulcher" on Greek Orthodox Patriarchate Road in the Christian quarter. They alone have a voice in the election of the patriarch. In the country, the clergy are mostly married and are chosen from the local Arab faithful.

According to the status quo imposed by the Ottomans in the middle of the nineteenth century, the Orthodox control most of the Basilicas of the Holy Sepulcher and the Nativity, even the candle concessions.

The Roman Catholic Church is open to intercommunion with the Orthodox churches, but the openness is not mutual, especially with the Greek Orthodox in Jerusalem. Test the waters before you attempt to communicate, lest you be embarrassed or insulted.

Patriarchs

In the Hebrew Scriptures the title "patriarch" is reserved exclusively for Abraham, his son, Isaac, his grandson Jacob (Israel), and twelve great-grandsons who are the founding fathers of the twelve tribes.

In Christian terminology it originally referred to the heads of those churches that had an apostle as a founding father. In the East, the power of the title was diminished when it was assumed by the head of any national church. The West followed a similar path by conferring it upon churches of great distinction and sometimes a nebulous connection with an apostle or evangelist such as Venice.

In Jerusalem, the Latin, Greek, and Armenian churches all claim the title for their archbishops as successors to St. James, bishop of Jerusalem.

Palestinians

Philistines or the peoples of the Sea arrived in the land of Canaan shortly before the Hebrews did. Eventually when it became a part of the Roman Empire, it received the name Palestine, after them. The name perdured during Byzantine, Arab, Crusader, Ottoman, and British rule. Today's inhabitants are descended from them, as well as from the ancient Canaanites. They are frequently called Arabs, but that arises more from the language they speak than from their ethnic identity. When the British took over the Palestinian Mandate from the League of Nations, the inhabitants for the first time looked forward to ruling their own country. That hope was diminished when the state of Israel was established, and the land that the Israelis did not occupy was annexed by the state of Jordan. Hundreds of thousands of Palestinians fled their homes and even their homeland in 1948 and 1967, becoming the Palestinian refugees. One day there will be the nation of Palestine alongside the nation of Israel. Inshallah! (God willing!). May justice and peace prevail for all.

Samaritans

The twelve tribes of Israel achieved unity only under three messiahs: Saul, David, and Solomon. Under Solomon's son Rehoboam, a schism ensued (circa 900 B.C.) leaving him with only the tribes of Benjamin and Judah in the south. The ten tribes of the north became the kingdom of Israel, eventually establishing its capital in Samaria. In 722–721 the northern kingdom was conquered by Assyria after a futile attempt at a revolution (cf. Isaiah 7; 2 Kings 15:28ff.). The Assyrians deported (the proverbial "lost ten tribes of Israel") all who might be possible leaders in a future revolt, and replaced them with captives from other conquered nations. The Samaritans are the offspring of these two groups of conquered peoples.

Considered schismatic, with their own place of worship on Mount Gerizim and heretical for accepting only the first five books of the Bible, they were cordially despised by and constantly feuded with their brother and sister Israelites in Judah and Jerusalem (cf. Sir 50:26). Jesus' opponents could think of no worse insult than to accuse him of being a Samaritan, possessed by a devil (John 8:48), and Jesus reciprocated by presenting the "Good Samaritan" as the neighbor who lived the commandment of love (Luke 10:25ff.).

Today the Samaritan high priest still offers the Passover sacrifice on Mount Gerizim and leads a community that numbers less than five hundred. Stung by the Jewish accusation of mixed blood, they now only marry among themselves, and the rate of birth defects is inordinately high.

Appendix III

FURTHER READING

There is no substitute for an attentive, prayerful reading of the Gospels in preparing for and following up on a pilgrimage. Almost any English edition will do but the study editions of the New American Bible and the Jerusalem Bible will reward those who are serious in hearing God's word. Use the introductions, the footnotes, and the cross references. Find out what the inspired author first intended to say to the early Christians of his community, and then ask how God is challenging you today through his word.

For further Scripture study, Princeton University's Bernhard W. Anderson has revised several times his invaluable *Understanding the Old Testament* (Prentice Hall). The superb *Introduction to the New Testament* by the renowned late Scripture scholar Raymond Brown, in the Anchor Bible series is all that one could wish for as a companion and guide through the Christian Scriptures.

For a popular appreciation of archaeology, James Michener's *The Source* can be enjoyable and enlightening. But for a *vade mecum,* there is nothing to compare with Jerome Murphy-O'Connor's *The Holy Land, An Archaeological Guide from Earliest Times to 1700* (Fourth ed., 1998, Oxford University Press). The author, a Dominican, is a long-time resident of Jerusalem and world-renowned biblical scholar and professor at the Ecole Biblique. Princeton University has published a fine reference book by Jack Finegan: *The Archaeology of the New Testament, The Life of Jesus and the Beginning of the Early Church*. A monk of the Dormition Abbey, Dom Bargil Pixner, has published the fruits of his research and archaeological work in his two volumes, *With Jesus through Galilee* (Collegeville: The Liturgical Press) and *With Jesus in Jerusalem* (Corazin, Israel).

Among periodicals, *Near Eastern Archaeology* (formerly *Biblical Archaeologist*) from the American Schools of Oriental Research is tops. The *Biblical Archaeological Review* has interesting articles concealed by the interminable advertisements, inane correspondence, and endless polemics.

As this guide goes to press, the first issue of a fine, new magazine is just off the press: *The World of the Bible.* If it lives up to its promise, it will fill a real need and will delight pilgrims who desire to learn the history, art, and archaeology of the Bible. It is available through Bayard Press, 90 Park Avenue, Suite 1600, New York, NY 10116 ($24.95 a year).

The Holy Land, a magazine published by the Franciscan Custody of the Holy Land, can be very useful for continuing the spirit of pilgrimage. It is available through them at 1400 Quincy St. N.E., Washington, D.C. 20017.

Browsing through back issues or the index of the *National Geographic* Society Magazine can be very rewarding. In recent years there have been articles as interesting and diverse as on the Palestinians, the Crusades, and the water crisis in the Middle East.

O Jerusalem by Larry Collins and Dominique LaPierre is gripping reading about the rise of Zionism and the establishment of the state of Israel. John W. Mulhall, C.S.P., has published *America and the Founding of Israel* (Los Angeles: Deshon Press). It answers many questions about the rights of Palestinian and Jew, the causes of the tensions, as well as an interpretation of the pertinent facts, statistics, and documents.

The novels of Chaim Potok, such as *In the Beginning* and *The Chosen* provide a fine appreciation for Orthodox Judaism, and the struggle of a young generation to come to grips with modern culture and education.

Videos: any number of travelogues on the Holy Land or Israel are available from libraries or video stores. My own video, more in the nature of a reflective pilgrimage using the words of Scripture and an explanation of them, was produced by Franciscan Communications and is marketed by St. Anthony Messenger Press. "The Birth of Jesus," "Jesus the Prophet," and "Jesus the Redeemer" are available separately or all three on one cassette: *Seeking Jesus in His Own Land.*

Appendix IV

ITEMS OF INTEREST

Ͳ

The Greek letters *Tau* and *Phi* are the abbreviation for tomb or sepulcher: TAPHOS. It is found as the sign of ownership on the properties of the Greek Orthodox.

The Cosmic Cross is also called the Holy Land Cross or the Franciscan Cross or the Crusaders' Cross. It has been said to represent the five wounds of Christ or the five nations of the Crusaders. Recent research indicates that it signifies the Gospel of the crucified and risen Lord being carried to the four corners of the universe. Today it is used to mark the sphere of influence or the property of the Latin Church.

Museums

The rewarding collections of the Israel Museum with its Shrine of the Book, housing the Dead Sea Scrolls, The Rockefeller Museum in East Jerusalem, and the Museum of the city of Jerusalem at Jaffa Gate are all well described in other guide books and a visit to one or all is rewarding. Other less-known museums which are just as interesting but less time-consuming are those of the Hebrew Union College Jewish Institute of Religion near the King David Hotel, the Holy Lands Museum near the Israel Museum, the Franciscan Biblical School of the Flagellation at the first station, the museums of the Greek Orthodox and Armenian Patriarchates, and the museum containing the finds from the excavations at Nazareth, adjacent to the Basilica.

The Name of God

In Exodus 3, when God reveals his name to Moses, he obviously wants that name to be known and invoked. It is Yahweh, a form of the verb "to be." This verb in Hebrew connotes much more than mere presence or existence. It is a presence which is dynamic, saving, and even creative. It tells us not only who God is, but also how God is related to us.

Unfortunately, a later generation misunderstood the second commandment and the divine name, Yahweh, was invoked only by the High Priest on the Day of Atonement in the seclusion of the Holy of Holies. Written Hebrew has no vowels, so when the language was no longer a living, spoken language (after 587 B.C.) vowels had to be added. The editors, knowing that wherever Y H W H (Yahweh) appeared in the text the reader was to read adonai or Lord in place of the Holy Name, inserted the vowels of Adonai between the consonants of Yahweh. They were never meant to be read together as those who refer to God as Jehovah mistakenly hold. There is no such name, title, or word.

Most English translations translate as Lord what the inspired biblical authors wrote as Yahweh. The Jerusalem Bible rightly retains the original usage of Yahweh, rather than the later circumlocution of Adonai or Lord.

Chronology

For those used to B.C. and A.D., the Israeli formulae of B.C.E. (before the common era) and C.E. (common era) may be surprising. No problem. The numbers still refer to the pivotal event of history: the birth of Jesus Christ.

Hymns

1. Abba! Father!

Refrain:
Abba, Abba, Father.
You are the potter;
we are the clay,
the work of your hands

Mold us, mold us and fashion us
into the image
of Jesus, your Son,
of Jesus, your Son. *(Refrain)*

Father, may we be one in you.
May we be one in you
as he is in you,
and you are in him. *(Refrain)*

Glory, glory and praise to you.
Glory and praise to you
forever, amen,
forever, amen. *(Refrain)*

Text: © 1977, Carey Landry and North American Liturgy Resources (NALR),
5536 NE Hassalo, Portland, OR 97213. All rights reserved. Used with permission.

2. Alleluia! Sing to Jesus

Alleluia! sing to Jesus!
His the scepter, his the throne;
Alleluia! his the triumph,

His the victory alone;
Hark! the songs of peaceful Zion
Thunder like a mighty flood;
Jesus out of every nation
Has redeemed us by his blood.

Alleluia! King eternal,
Thee the Lord of lords we own;
Alleluia! born of Mary
Earth thy footstool, heav'n thy throne:
You, within the veil, have entered,
Robed in flesh, our great high priest;
Here on earth both priest and victim
In the eucharistic feast.

Text: Rev 5:9, William Chatterton Dix, 1837–98.

3. Amazing Grace

Amazing grace! how sweet the sound,
That saved a soul like me!
I once was lost, but now am found,
Was blind, but now I see.

'Twas grace that taught my heart to fear,
And grace my fears relieved;
How precious did that grace appear
The hour I first believed!
The Lord has promised good to me,
His word my hope secures;
He will my shield and portion be
As long as life endures.

Through many dangers, toils, and snares,
I have already come;
'Tis grace that brought me safe thus far,
And grace will lead me home.

Text: John Newton, 1725–1807.

4. At the Cross Her Station Keeping

At the cross her station keeping,
Mary stood in sorrow, weeping,
When her son was crucified.

While she waited in her anguish,
Seeing Christ in torment languish,
Bitter sorrow pierced her heart.

Mary, fount of love's devotion,
Let me share with true emotion
All the sorrow you endured.

Let me to your love be taken,
Let my soul in death awaken
To the joys of Paradise.

Text ascribed to Jacapone da Todi, translated by Anthony G. Petti © 1971 by Faber Music Limited.
Reprinted from NEW CATHOLIC HYMNAL by permission of the publishers.

5. Battle Hymn of the Republic (Mine Eyes Have Seen the Glory)

Mine eyes have seen the glory of the coming of the Lord;
He is trampling out the vintage where the grapes of wrath are stored;
He has loosed the fateful lightning of his terrible swift sword;
His truth is marching on.

Refrain:
Glory! Glory! Hallelujah! Glory! Glory! Hallelujah!
Glory! Glory! Hallelujah! His truth is marching on.

In the beauty of the lilies Christ was born across the sea,
With a glory in his bosom that transfigures you and me;
As he died to make us holy, let us die that all be free!
While God is marching on. *(Refrain)*

Text: Julia W. Howe, 1819–1910.

6. Be Not Afraid

You shall cross the barren desert, but you shall not die of thirst;
You shall wander far in safety, though you do not know the way.
You shall speak your words in foreign lands, and all will understand.
You shall see the face of God and live.

Refrain:
Be not afraid; I go before you always.
Come, follow me, and I will give you rest.

If you pass through raging waters in the sea, you shall not drown.
If you walk amid the burning flames, you shall not be harmed.
If you stand before the power of hell and death is at your side,
Know that I am with you through it all. *(Refrain)*

Blessed are your poor, for the kingdom shall be theirs;
Blest are you that weep and mourn, for one day you will laugh;
And if wicked ones insult and hate you all because of me,
Blessed, blessed are you. *(Refrain)*

Text: Robert J. Dufford, s.j., 1943.

7. Christ Be Beside Me (Prayer of St. Patrick)

Christ be beside me, Christ be before me,
Christ be behind me, King of my heart.
Christ be within me, Christ be below me,
Christ be above me, never to part.

Christ on my right hand, Christ on my left hand,
Christ all around me, shield in the strife.
Christ in my sleeping, Christ in my sitting,
Christ in my rising, light of my life.

Christ be in all hearts thinking about me;
Christ be on all tongues telling me.
Christ be the vision in eyes that see me;
In ears that hear me, Christ ever be.

Text: Trans. James D. Quinn, s.j. © 1969, James D. Quinn, s.j.,
by permission of Selah Publishing Co., Kingston, NY.

8. The Church's One Foundation

The Church's one foundation
Is Jesus Christ her Lord:
She is his new creation,
Through water and the word.
From heaven he came and sought her
To be his holy bride;
With his own blood he bought her,
And for her life he died.

Elect from every nation
Yet one o'er all the earth,
Her charter of salvation
One Lord, one faith, one birth,
One holy name she blesses,
Partakes one holy food,
And to one hope she presses,
With ev'ry grace endued.

The Church on earth hath union
With God the Three in One,
And holy graced communion
With those whose rest is won.
O happy saints and holy!
Lord give us strength that we
Like them, the meek and lowly,
may dwell on high with thee.

Text: Samuel John Stone, 1839–1900.

9. Come, Holy Ghost

Come, Holy Ghost, Creator blest,
And in our hearts take up thy rest;
Come with thy grace and heav'nly aid
To fill the hearts which thou hast made,
To fill the hearts which thou hast made.

O Comforter, to thee we cry,
Thou heav'nly gift of God most high;
Thou fount of life, and fire of love,
And sweet anointing from above,
And sweet anointing from above.

Text: Veni, Creator Spiritus: attr. to Rabanus Maurus, 776–856;
trans. Edward Caswall, 1814–78.

10. Crown Him with Many Crowns

Crown him with many crowns,
The Lamb upon his throne;
Hark! How the heav'nly anthem drowns
All music but its own.

Awake, my soul, and sing
Of him who set us free,
And hail him as your heav'nly King
Through all eternity.

Text: Rev 19:12, Matthew Bridges, 1800–94.

11. Hail, Holy Queen Enthroned Above

Hail, holy Queen enthroned above, O Maria.
Hail, Queen of mercy and of love, O Maria.
Triumph, all ye Cherubim,
Sing with us, ye Seraphim,
Heav'n and earth resound the hymn:
Salve, Salve, Salve, Regina.

Our life, our sweetness here below, O Maria.
Our hope in sorrow and in woe, O Maria.
Triumph, all ye Cherubim,
Sing with us, ye Seraphim,
Heav'n and earth resound the hymn:
Salve, Salve, Salve, Regina.

Text: Hermanus Contractus, 1013–54; trans. anon., ca. 1884.

12. Hail Mary, Gentle Woman

Introduction (solo):
Hail Mary, full of grace, the Lord is with you,
Blessed are you among women,
and blessed is the fruit of your womb, Jesus.
Holy Mary, mother of God, pray for us sinners now
And at the hour of death. Amen.

Refrain:
Gentle woman, quiet light,
Morning star, so strong and bright,
Gentle Mother, peaceful dove,
Teach us wisdom; teach us love.

You were chosen by the Father,
You were chosen for the Son.
You were chosen from all women
And for woman, shining one. *(Refrain)*

Blessed are you among women,
Blest in turn all women, too.
Blessed they with peaceful spirits.
Blessed they with gentle hearts. *(Refrain)*

13. Hail, Redeemer, King Divine

Hail, redeemer, king divine!
Priest and lamb, the throne is thine;
King whose reign shall never cease,
Prince of everlasting peace.

Refrain:
Angels, saints and nations sing:
"Praised be Jesus Christ, our king;
Lord of earth and sky and sea,
King of love on Calvary."

King of everlasting might!
Be to us eternal light,
Till in peace each nation rings
With the praises, king of kings. *(Refrain)*

14. The Holy City

Last night I lay asleeping,
There came a dream so fair,
I stood in old Jerusalem,
Beside the Temple there.
I heard the children singing
And ever as they sang,
I thought the voice of angels
From heaven in answer rang.

Jerusalem, Jerusalem, lift up your gates and sing,
Hosanna in the highest, hosanna to your King.

And then I thought my dream was changed,
The streets no longer rang,

Hushed were the glad hosannas,
The little children sang.
The sun grew dark with mystery,
The earth was cold and chill
As the shadow of a cross arose
Upon a lonely hill.

Jerusalem, Jerusalem, hark, how the angels sing.
Hosanna in the highest, hosanna to your King.

And once again the scene was changed,
New earth there seemed to be.
I saw the holy city
Beside the tideless sea.
The light of God was on its streets,
The gates were opened wide;
And all who would might enter,
And no one was denied.
No need of moon or stars by night
Or sun to shine by day,
It was the new Jerusalem
That will not pass away.

Jerusalem, Jerusalem, sing for the night is o'er;
Hosanna in the highest, hosanna forevermore.

Text: Stephen Adam, 1892.

15. Holy God, We Praise Thy Name

Holy God, we praise thy name!
Lord of all, we bow before thee;
All on earth thy scepter claim,
All in heav'n above adore thee;
Infinite thy vast domain,
Everlasting is thy reign.

Hark! the loud celestial hymn
Angel choirs above are raising;
Cherubim and Seraphim
In unceasing chorus praising,
Fill the heav'ns with sweet accord:
Holy, holy, holy Lord!

Fill the heav'ns with sweet accord:
Holy, holy, holy Lord!

Text: Ignaz Franz, 1719–90; trans. Clarence A. Walworth, 1820–1900.

16. Holy, Holy, Holy! Lord God Almighty

Holy, Holy, Holy! Lord God Almighty!
Early in the morning our song shall rise to thee:
Holy, Holy, Holy! merciful and mighty,
God in three Persons, blessed Trinity.

Holy, Holy, Holy! all the saints adore thee,
Casting down their golden crowns around the glassy sea;
Cherubim and seraphim falling down before thee,
God everlasting through eternity.

Holy, Holy, Holy! though the darkness hide thee,
Though the eye made blind by sin thy glory may not see,
Only thou art holy; there is none beside thee,
Perfect in power, in love, in purity.

Text: Reginald Heber, 1783–1826.

17. How Great Thou Art

O Lord my God, when I in awesome wonder
Consider all the worlds Thy hands have made,
I see the stars, I hear the rolling thunder,
Thy pow'r throughout the universe displayed!

Refrain:
Then sings my soul, my Savior God, to Thee;
How great Thou art, how great Thou art!
Then sings my soul, my Savior God, to Thee;
How great Thou art, how great Thou art!

When through the woods and forest glades I wander
And hear the birds sing sweetly in the trees,
When I look down from lofty mountain grandeur
And hear the brook and feel the gentle breeze. *(Refrain)*

And when I think that God, His Son not sparing,
Sent Him to die, I scarce can take it in
That on the cross, my burden gladly bearing,
He bled and died to take away my sin! *(Refrain)*

Christ Jesus Lord, you rose that Easter morning,
And to your friends you came to show the way.
Shalom my gift, again I say shalom,
Abba's spirit is yours this blessed day. *(Refrain)*

When Christ shall come with shout of acclamation
And take me home, what joy shall fill my heart!
Then I shall bow in humble adoration
And there proclaim, my God, how great Thou art! *(Refrain)*

18. I Am the Bread of Life

I am the Bread of life.
You who come to me shall not hunger;
And who believe in me shall not thirst.
No one can come to me
Unless the Father beckons.

Refrain:
And I will raise you up,
And I will raise you up,
And I will raise you up on the last day.

The bread that I will give
Is my flesh for the life of the world,
And if you eat of this bread,
You shall live forever,
You shall live forever. *(Refrain)*

I am the Resurrection,
I am the life.
If you believe in me,
Even though you die,
You shall live forever. *(Refrain)*

19. The King of Glory

Refrain:
The King of glory comes, the nation rejoices.
Open the gates before him, lift up your voices.

Who is the king of glory; how shall we call him?
He is Emmanuel, the promised of ages. *(Refrain)*

Sing then of David's Son, our Savior and brother;
In all of Galilee was never another. *(Refrain)*

Text: © 1966, 1984, Willard F. Jabusch. Used by permission.

20. Let All That Is Within Me

Refrain:
Let all that is within me cry holy;
Let all that is within me cry holy.

Holy, holy, holy is the Lamb that was slain. *(Refrain)*

Glory to the Lamb that was slain. *(Refrain)*

Jesus is the lamb that was slain. *(Refrain)*

Text: Author unknown.

21. Let Us Break Bread Together

Let us break bread together on our knees;
Let us break bread together on our knees.

Refrain:
When I fall on my knees,
with my face to the rising sun,
O Lord, have mercy on me.

Let us drink wine together on our knees;
Let us drink wine together on our knees. *(Refrain)*

Let us praise God together on our knees;
Let us praise God together on our knees. *(Refrain)*

Text: American folk hymn.

22. Lift High the Cross

Refrain:
Lift high the cross, the love of Christ proclaim
Till all the world adore his sacred name.

Come, Christians, follow where your Savior trod;
Our King victorious, Christ the Son of God. *(Refrain)*

O Lord, once lifted on the glorious tree,
As thou once promised, draw us all to thee. *(Refrain)*

So shall our shout of triumph ever be.
Praise to the Lord of life for victory. *(Refrain)*

23. Like a Shepherd

Refrain:
Like a shepherd he feeds his flock
And gathers the lambs in his arms,
Holding them carefully close to his heart,
Leading them home.

Say to the cities of Judah;
Prepare the way of the Lord.
Go to the mountaintop, lift your voice:
Jerusalem, here is your God. *(Refrain)*

I myself will shepherd them,
For others have led them astray.
The lost I will rescue and heal their wounds
And pasture them, giving them rest. *(Refrain)*

24. Magnificat
(to the tune of Amazing Grace)

Magnificat, magnificat
Magnificat, Praise God!
Magnificat, magnificat,
Magnificat, Praise God!

My soul proclaims the Lord my God,
My spirit sings his praise.
He looks on me, he lifts me up,
And gladness fills my days.

All nations now will share my joy,
His gifts he has outpoured.
His little ones he has made great,
I magnify the Lord.

For those who love his holy name,
His mercy will not die,
His strong right arm
Puts down the proud,
And lifts the lowly high.

He fills the hungry with good things;
The rich he sends away.
The promise made to Abraham
Is filled to endless day.

Text: Author unknown.

25. Peace Prayer of St. Francis (Make Me a Channel of Your Peace)

Make me a channel of your peace.
Where there is hatred, let me bring your love.
Where there is injury, your pardon, Lord,
And where there's doubt, true faith in you.

Make me a channel of your peace.
Where there's despair in life, let me bring hope.
Where there is darkness, only light,
And where there's sadness, ever joy.

Oh, Master, grant that I may never seek
So much to be consoled as to console.
To be understood as to understand.
To be loved as to love with all my soul.

Make me a channel of your peace.
It is in pardoning that we are pardoned,
In giving of ourselves that we receive,
And in dying that we're born to eternal life.

Text: Prayer of St. Francis; adapt. by Sebastian Temple, 1928. Dedicated to Mrs. Frances Tracy.
© 1967, OCP Publications, 5536 NE Hassalo, Portland, OR 97213.
All rights reserved. Used with permission.

26. Sing a New Song

Refrain:
Sing a new song unto the Lord;
Let your song be sung from mountains high.
Sing a new song unto the Lord,
Singing alleluia.

Yahweh's people dance for joy.
O come before the Lord.
And play for him on glad tambourines,
And let your trumpet sound. *(Refrain)*

Rise, O children, from your sleep;
Your Savior now has come.
He has turned your sorrow to joy,
And filled your soul with song. *(Refrain)*

Glad my soul for I have seen
The glory of the Lord.
The trumpet sounds; the dead shall be raised.
I know my Savior lives. *(Refrain)*

27. Sing of Mary

Sing of Mary, pure and lowly,
Virgin mother undefiled.
Sing of God's own Son most holy,
Who became her little child.
Fairest child of fairest mother,
God the Lord who came to earth.
Word made flesh our very brother,
Takes our nature by his birth.

Sing of Jesus, Son of Mary,
In the home at Nazareth.
Toil and labor cannot weary,
Love enduring unto death.
Constant was the love he gave her,

Though he went forth from her side;
Forth to preach and heal and suffer,
Till on Calvary he died.

Text: Roland F. Palmer, 1891–1985.

28. Sing to the Mountains

Refrain:
Sing to the mountains, sing to the sea.
Raise your voices, lift your hearts.
This is the day the Lord has made.
Let all the earth rejoice.

I will give thanks to you, my Lord.
You have answered my plea.
You have saved my soul from death.
You are my strength and my song. *(Refrain)*

Holy, holy, holy Lord,
Heaven and earth are full of your glory. *(Refrain)*

This is the day that the Lord has made.
Let us be glad and rejoice.
He has turned all death to life.
Sing of the glory of God. *(Refrain)*

Text: Psalm 118; Bob Dufford, s.j., 1943. © 1975, Robert J. Dufford, s.j.,
and New Dawn Music, 5536 NE Hassalo, Portland, OR 97213.
All rights reserved. Used with permission.

29. Were You There When They Crucified My Lord?

Were you there when they crucified my Lord?
Were you there when they crucified my Lord?
O! Sometimes it causes me to tremble, tremble, tremble.
Were you there when they crucified my Lord?

Were you there when they nailed him to the tree?
Were you there when they nailed him to the tree?
O! Sometimes it causes me to tremble, tremble, tremble.
Were you there when they nailed him to the tree?

Were you there when they laid him in the tomb?
Were you there when they laid him in the tomb?
O! Sometimes it causes me to tremble, tremble, tremble.
Were you there when they laid him in the tomb?

Were you there when he rose up from the grave?
Were you there when he rose up from the grave?
O! Sometimes it causes me to tremble, tremble, tremble.
Were you there when he rose up from the grave?

Text: African-American spiritual.

30. Whatsoever You Do

Refrain:
Whatsoever you do to the least of my people,
that you do unto me.

When I was hungry, you gave me to eat;
When I was thirsty, you gave me to drink.
Now enter into the home of my Father. *(Refrain)*

When I was weary, you helped me find rest;
When I was anxious, you calmed all my fears.
Now enter into the home of my Father. *(Refrain)*

You saw me covered with spittle and blood;
You knew my features, though grimy with sweat.
Now enter into the home of my Father. *(Refrain)*

When I was laughed at, you stood by my side;
When I was happy, you shared in my joy.
Now enter into the home of my Father. *(Refrain)*

Text: © 1966, 1982, Willard F. Jabusch. Used by permission.

31. Yes, I Shall Arise

Refrain:
Yes, I shall arise and return to my Father!

To you, O Lord, I lift up my soul;
In you, O my God, I place all my trust. *(Refrain)*

My heart and soul shall yearn for your face;
Be gracious to me and answer my plea. *(Refrain)*

Give me again the joy of your help;
Now open my lips, your praise I will sing. *(Refrain)*

You are my joy, my refuge and strength;
Let all upright hearts give praise to the Lord. *(Refrain)*

My soul will sing, my heart will rejoice;
The blessings of God will fill all my days. *(Refrain)*

32. You Satisfy the Hungry Heart

Refrain:
You satisfy the hungry heart
With gift of finest wheat;
Come give to us,
O saving Lord,
The bread of life to eat.

As when the shepherd calls his sheep,
They know and heed his voice;
So when you call your fam'ly Lord,
We follow and rejoice. *(Refrain)*

You give yourself to us, O Lord;
Then selfless let us be,
To serve each other in your name
In truth and charity. *(Refrain)*

The above hymns were chosen because they are widely known and suitable
for one or more of the Holy Places. The director should peruse the list and
add others that the group may know, e.g., *All Hail the Power of Jesus' Name;*
Alleluia, the Strife is Oe'r; Be Thou My Vision; Jesus Christ Is Risen Today;
Joyful, Joyful, We Adore Thee; Let Us Break Bread Together, etc.

Christmas Carols

1. Angels We Have Heard on High

Angels we have heard on high,
Sweetly singing o'er the plains;
And the mountains in reply,
Echoing their joyous strains.

Refrain:
Gloria in excelsis deo, gloria in excelsis deo.

Shepherds, why this jubilee?
Why your gladsome strains prolong?
Say what may the tidings be
Which inspire your heav'nly song? *(Refrain)*

Come to Bethlehem and see
Him whose birth the angels sing;
Come adore on bended knee,
Christ the Lord, the newborn king. *(Refrain)*

Text: Traditional French carol.

2. Hark! The Herald Angels Sing

Hark! the herald angels sing,
"Glory to the newborn King;
Peace on earth, and mercy mild
God and sinners reconciled!"

Joyful, all you nations, rise,
Join the triumph of the skies;
With angelic host proclaim,
"Christ is born in Bethlehem!"

Refrain:
Hark! the herald angels sing,
"Glory to the newborn King!"

What good news the angels bring,
What glad tidings of our King.
Christ the Lord is born today,
Christ who takes our sins away.
He who rules both heaven and earth,
Has in Bethlehem his birth.
With th' angelic host proclaim, Christ is born in Bethlehem. *(Refrain)*

Glory be to God on high,
Peace to all God's people on earth.
O Lord God, almighty King,
We praise you and we give you thanks.
Jesus Christ, God's only Son,
You are Lord, the Lamb of God.
You have freed us from our sins,
Hear our prayer and grant us peace. *(Refrain)*

Christ by highest heav'n adored,
Christ the everlasting Lord.
You alone are holy Lord,
You alone are God most high.
Holy, holy, holy One,
Glory be to you alone.
Lord of all to you we raise,
This our hymn of joyful praise. *(Refrain)*

Text: first two verses by Charles Wesley, 1707–88.

3. Joy to the World

Joy to the world! the Lord is come:
Let earth receive her King;
Let ev'ry heart prepare him room,

And heav'n and nature sing,
And heav'n and nature sing,
And heav'n, and heav'n and nature sing.

Joy to the world! the Savior reigns:
Let us, our songs employ;
While fields and floods, rocks, hills and plains
Repeat the sounding joy,
Repeat the sounding joy,
Repeat, repeat the sounding joy.

Glory to God, the sounding skies,
With joy their anthems ring;
Peace to the earth, good will to all
From heav'n's eternal King,
From heav'n's eternal King,
From heav'n's, from heav'n's eternal King.

Text: vv. 1 and 2, Isaac Watts, 1674–1748; v. 3, E. H. Sears, 1876.

4. O Come, All Ye Faithful

O come, all ye faithful, joyful and triumphant,
O come ye, O come ye to Bethlehem;
Come and behold him, born the King of angels.

Refrain:
O come, let us adore him, O come let us adore him,
O come, let us adore him, Christ the Lord!

Sing, choirs of angels, sing in exultation,
Sing, all ye citizens of heav'n above!
Glory to God, all glory in the highest. *(Refrain)*

Text: John F. Wade, ca. 1711–86; trans. Frederick Oakeley, 1802–80.

5. O Come, O Come, Emmanuel

O come, O come, Emmanuel,
And ransom captive Israel,
That mourns in lonely exile here
Until the Son of God appear.

Refrain:
Rejoice! Rejoice! Emmanuel
Shall come to you, O Israel.

O come, thou dayspring from on high,
And cheer us by thy drawing nigh.
Disperse the gloomy clouds of night,
And death's dark shadow put to flight. *(Refrain)*

O come, desire of nations, bind
In one the hearts of humankind;
O bid our sad divisions cease,
And be for us our King of Peace. *(Refrain)*

Text: trans. John M. Neale, 1818–66.

6. Silent Night, Holy Night

Silent night, holy night!
All is calm, all is bright
Round yon Virgin
Mother and Child.
Holy Infant so tender and mild,
Sleep in heavenly peace,
Sleep in heavenly peace.

Silent night, holy night!
Shepherds quake at the sight!
Glories stream from heaven afar,
Heav'nly hosts sing alleluia.
Christ, the Savior, is born,
Christ, the Savior, is born.

Silent night, holy night!
Son of God, love's pure light,
Radiant beams from thy holy face,
With the dawn of redeeming grace.
Jesus Lord, at thy birth,
Jesus Lord, at thy birth.

Text: Joseph Mohr, 1792–1849; trans. John F. Young, 1820–85.

7. We Three Kings of Orient Are

We three kings of Orient are,
Bearing gifts we traverse afar
Field and fountain,

Moor and mountain,
Following yonder star.

Refrain:
O star of wonder, star of night,
Star with royal beauty bright,
Westward leading, still proceeding,
Guide us to the perfect Light.

Glorious now behold him rise,
King and God and sacrifice:
Heav'n sings, "Hallelujah!"
"Hallelujah!" earth replies. *(Refrain)*

Text: John H. Hopkins Jr., 1820–91.

(Other carols: *Away in a Manger; It Came upon the Midnight Clear; O Holy Night; O Little Town of Bethlehem; The First Nowell; What Child Is This?*

Index